PASSWORD 1

A Reading and Vocabulary Text

Linda Butler

Longman

For Jim, Miles, and Clare, with thanks for their love and support

Password 1

Pearson Education, 10 Bank Street, White Plains, NY 10606

Vice president, director of instructional design: Allen Ascher
Development director: Penny Laporte
Senior acquisitions editor: Laura Le Dréan
Development editors: Stacey Hunter, Karen Davy
Vice president, director of design and production: Rhea Banker
Director of electronic production: Aliza Greenblatt
Executive managing editor: Linda Moser
Production manager: Ray Keating
Production editor: Sasha Kintzler
Art director: Patricia Wosczyk
Director of manufacturing: Patrice Fraccio
Senior manufacturing buyer: David Dickey
Photo research: Dana Klinek
Cover design: Tracey Cataldo
Text design: Ann France, Patricia Wosczyk
Digital layout specialist: Lisa Ghiozzi

ISBN: 0-13-110125-0
ISBN: 0-13-111152-3 (book with two audio CDs)

1 2 3 4 5 6 7 8 9 10—CRK—07 06 05 04 03 02

Printed in the United States of America

Contents

To the Teacher

The *Password* series is designed to help learners of English develop their reading skills and expand their vocabularies. Each book in the series offers theme-based units with engaging readings, a variety of activities to develop language skills, and exercises to help students understand, remember, and use new words.

Each book in the series can be used independently of the others. *Password 1* is for high beginners assumed to have an English vocabulary of about 600 words; *Password 2* assumes a vocabulary of about 1,000 words; and *Password 3*, about 1,500. With each book, students will learn about 500 new words and phrases, all of them high-frequency in American English. The *Password* series can help students reach the 2,000-word level in English, at which point, research has shown, most learners can handle basic everyday oral communication and begin to read unadapted texts. The vocabulary taught in the *Password* series has been carefully chosen. Target word choices have been based on analyses of authentic language data in various corpora, including data in the Longman Corpus Network, to determine which words are most frequently used and therefore most likely to be needed by students. Also targeted are common collocations and other multi-word units, including phrasal verbs. The target vocabulary is not determined by the topic of a chapter, but rather by the frequency and usefulness of the words across a range of subjects.

While becoming a good reader in English does involve more than knowing the meanings of words, there is no doubt that vocabulary is key. To learn new words, students need to see them repeatedly and in varied contexts. They must become skilled at guessing meaning from context but can do this successfully only when they understand the context. For that reason, the sentence structure and vocabulary in the readings have been carefully controlled. The vocabulary used in the readings is limited to those 600, 1,000, or 1,500 high-frequency words that the learner is assumed to know, plus the words and phrases targeted in the chapter and those recycled from previous chapters. The new vocabulary is explained and practiced in exercises and activities, encountered again in later readings and tasks, and reviewed in oral drills and self-tests. This emphasis on systematic vocabulary acquisition is a highlight of the *Password* series.

INTRODUCTION TO *PASSWORD 1*

Password 1 is intended for high beginning students. It assumes a vocabulary of about 600 English words and teaches about 500 more. From 12 to 15 words and phrases from each reading passage are targeted in the exercises for that chapter and recycled in later chapters. Because of the systematic building of vocabulary, as well as the progression of reading skills exercises, it is best to do the units and chapters in the order they appear in the book.

Most of the target words are among the 1,000 most high-frequency words in English—the vocabulary students need to build a solid foundation of English.

Others have been targeted for their usefulness in discussing the theme, such as *career* and *profession* in Unit Four: Working.

Organization of the Book

The book contains seven units, each with four chapters followed by a Wrap-up section. After Units Four and Seven, there are Vocabulary Self-Tests. At the end of the book you will find the Vocabulary Self-Tests Answer Key and the Index to Target Words and Phrases.

THE UNITS   Each unit is based on a theme and includes four readings that deal with real people, places, and events. Students need to understand, discuss, and write about the content, but they are not expected to memorize it.

THE CHAPTERS   Each of the four chapters within a unit is organized as follows:

Getting Ready to Read   Each chapter opens with a photo or illustration and pre-reading questions or tasks. These are often for pair or small group work but may be best handled as a full-class activity when students need more guidance. *Getting Ready to Read* starts students thinking about the subject of the reading by drawing on what they already know, eliciting their opinions, and/or introducing relevant vocabulary.

Reading   This section contains the reading passage for the chapter. These passages progress from about 200 to about 450 words by the end of the book. In the first three units, only present and future tense verbs are used; the simple past tense, introduced in Unit Four, is the only other verb tense students will encounter. Students should do the reading the first time without dictionaries. You may wish to have them reread while you read aloud or play the audio, as listening while reading can be helpful to students' comprehension and retention. It is also helpful for students to hear the pronunciation of new words. The reading is followed by *Quick Comprehension Check,* a brief true/false exercise that lets students check their general understanding. It is a good idea to go over the *Quick Comprehension Check* statements in class. When a statement is true, you may want to ask students how they know it is true; when it is false, have students correct it. By doing so, you send them back into the reading to find support for their answers. Try to avoid spending time explaining vocabulary at this point.

Exploring Vocabulary   Once students have a general understanding of the reading, it is time to focus on new words. In *Thinking about the Vocabulary,* students are asked to look at the list of Target Words and Phrases and circle (both on the list and in the reading) those that are new to them. Then they reread, noticing the uses of these particular words. From the beginning, they are asked to examine the context of each unknown word and see what information the context gives them. They will probably need to work on this first as a whole class, with your guidance; later they can discuss new word meanings in pairs. *Using the Vocabulary* follows, with three exercises of various types, to help students understand the meanings of the target vocabulary as used in the reading and in other contexts. These exercises can be done in or out of class by students working individually or in pairs. In *Building on the Vocabulary,* you will find a word grammar or collocation exercise. Grammar exercises include study of the most common parts of speech, phrasal verbs, noncount nouns, and irregular past tense forms. The collocation exercises focus students' attention on how words combine with others, given that knowing about possible word combinations (for example, knowing that *do,* not *make,* goes with homework) is an important aspect of learning new vocabulary. Only after working through all the exercises in *Exploring New Vocabulary* should students turn to their dictionaries for further information, if needed.

Developing Your Skills   In this section are tasks that require students to focus again on the reading. The exercises include work on scanning, answering comprehension questions, summarizing, recognizing cause and effect, focusing on details, determining pronoun reference, and identifying or stating the main idea. You will also find a fluency-building exercise: *Discussion, Sharing Opinions, Role-playing,* or *Interviewing.* The exercise *Using New Words* has pairs of students working productively with the target vocabulary orally and/or in writing. The chapter ends with *Writing,* where students are asked to write sentences or paragraphs. Sometimes there will be a choice of two or more topics related to the content of the reading. How you wish to use these writing tasks will depend on your goals for the course.

THE UNIT WRAP-UPS   Each unit ends with a four-part Wrap-up section that brings together the vocabulary from the four chapters. The unit Wrap-up provides a key follow-up to the initial learning of the vocabulary—to consolidate and enrich students' understanding of new words. The first part is *Reviewing Vocabulary,* with varied exercises to review word meanings; the second is *Expanding on Vocabulary,* with exercises on word families, word parts, and collocations; the third is *Playing with Words,* a crossword or word search puzzle; and the fourth is *Building Dictionary Skills,* using excerpts from the *Longman Dictionary of American English.*

THE VOCABULARY SELF-TESTS   Two multiple choice vocabulary tests appear in the book, the first covering Units 1–4, the second Units 5–7. The answers are given on page 246. (Unit tests can be found in the Teacher's Manual.)

THE TEACHER'S MANUAL

The Teacher's Manual for *Password 1* contains:

• Answer key for all exercises in the book

• Seven unit tests with answers

• Quick Oral Review, sets of prompts you can use for rapid drills of vocabulary studied in previous chapters. These drills can be an important part of the spaced repetition of vocabulary—repeated exposures to newly-learned words at increasing intervals—that helps students remember the words they learn. For tips on how to use the prompts, see the Introduction in the Teacher's Manual.

To the Student

Welcome to *Password 1!* This book will help you to read better in English and to learn many new words. You will read about real people, places, and things from around the world. I hope you have fun reading, writing, and talking about them.

Linda Butler

Acknowledgments

I would like to thank first the people who shared their stories with me so that students can enjoy them in this book: Ferdie Adoboe, Gilberto Conchas, Jad Davis, Marlin Fan, Laura Gilbert, Reyna Giner de Oriol, Tim Hoban, Vitek Kruta, Arunaa and Hervé Phalippou, Judith Prakash, Murat Sanal, and Ember Swift. Thanks also to my students at Saint Michael's College in Colchester, Vermont, and at Holyoke Community College in Holyoke, Massachusetts, for their helpful feedback on the materials. I would also like to thank the reviewers whose insightful comments on early drafts of this book were much appreciated:

Reviewers: **Hülya Akaslan,** Mehmet Akif Ersoy Anadolu Lisesi, Corlu, Turkey; **Charlotte Calobrisi,** Northern Virginia Community College, Annandale, VA; **Ann Carlson,** Intrax, San Francisco, CA; **Özden Ergül,** T.C. Maltepe University, Istanbul, Turkey; **Sally Gearhart,** Santa Rosa Junior College, Santa Rosa, CA; **Greg Goodmacher,** Kwassui College, Nagasaki, Japan; **Jóna Hammer,** Duquesne University, Pittsburgh, PA; **Susan Jamieson,** English Language Institute, Bellevue, WA; **Molly McGrath,** Hunter College, City University of New York, New York, NY; **Phoebe Rivera,** Los Angeles Mission College, Sylmar, CA; **Nina Rosen,** Santa Rosa Junior College, Santa Rosa, CA; **June Ohrnberger,** Suffolk County Community College, Brentwood, NY; **Alice Savage,** North Harris Community College, Houston, TX; **Kathy Sherak,** San Francisco State University, San Francisco, CA; **Melissa Torriero,** Capital Community College, Hartford, CT, and Ethel Walker School, Simsbury, CT; **Lorraine Villemaire,** Massachusetts Career Development Institute, Springfield, MA; **Rob Waring,** Notre Dame Seishin University, Okayama, Japan; **Linda Wells,** University of Washington, Seattle, WA; **Patricia Zebrowski,** Rutgers University, Piscataway, NJ; **Taurayi Zhante,** Kitazato University, Sagamihara, Japan.

A great many people at Longman helped in the making of this book, most of all, Laura Le Dréan, Senior Acquisitions Editor. Her experience as an editor and as a teacher, her good judgment and good humor, and her unfailing support were invaluable. I would also like to thank Allen Ascher, Vice President, Director of Instructional Design; Penny Laporte, Development Director; Stacey Hunter and Karen Davy, Development Editors; Mykan White and Dana Klinek, Editorial Assistants; Sasha Kintzler, Production Editor; and illustrators Jill Wood and Hillary Price.

L.B.

UNIT 1

FREE
TIME

CHAPTER 1

A Student and a Dancer

Reyna the dancer

GETTING READY TO READ

Talk with a partner.

1. Look at the young woman in the photo. Where do you think she is from?
2. Read the questions in the chart. Write your answers. Then ask your partner. Write your partner's answers.

	YOU	YOUR PARTNER
a. Do you like to dance?		
b. Do you like to watch people dancing?		
c. Do you like to listen to music?		
d. What kind of music or dancing do you like?		

READING

Look at the words and pictures next to the reading. Then read without stopping. Don't worry about new words. Don't stop to use a dictionary. Just keep reading!

A Student and a Dancer

1   Reyna Giner de Oriol is from Caracas, Venezuela. Right now, she is a student in the United States. Reyna is taking **courses** in **education** at an American college. She's planning to teach English back home in Venezuela.

2   **During** the school week, Reyna spends a lot of time at the college. Every day, she sits and listens in her classes, sits and reads in the **library**, and sits and works at a computer. At home in her apartment, she sits and studies at her **desk**. All this sitting is hard for Reyna. She doesn't like to sit—she likes to move!

3   In her free time, Reyna dances the flamenco. It's a **famous** dance from Spain. She dances to Spanish guitar[1] music. The music can be fast or slow. It can be happy, sad, or romantic.[2] Reyna says, "You can't just listen to the music— you have to feel it in your heart. Then you show your **feelings** in your dancing."

4   Reyna dances the flamenco with castanets[3] in her hands. She moves them with her **fingers**. "The hands are very important in the flamenco," she says. "I want my hands to look like a **pair** of flying birds."

5   These days,[4] Reyna doesn't dance very often. She's **busy** with schoolwork. She **misses** dancing. She sometimes talks about the flamenco with students from other countries. Sometimes she dances for them, too. "And every night, in my sleep," Reyna says, "I dance in my **dreams**."

[1] a *Spanish guitar*

[2] *romantic* = about love

[3] a pair of *castanets*

[4] *these days* = now

Quick Comprehension Check

Read these sentences. Circle T (true) or F (false).

1. Reyna is studying at a college in the United States. Ⓣ   F
2. She studies at school and at home.   T   F
3. She's taking classes in flamenco dancing.   T   F
4. Flamenco music is always fast and happy.   T   F
5. Flamenco dancers don't move their hands.   T   F
6. Reyna doesn't dance very often because of her schoolwork.   T   F

EXPLORING VOCABULARY

Thinking about the Vocabulary

Guessing Meaning from Context

We use words in a **context**. The context of a word is the words and sentences before and after it. These other words can help you guess a word's meaning. For example, look at the context of *library:*

> Reyna spends a lot of time at the college. Every day, she sits and listens in her classes, sits and reads in the **library**, . . .

The context of *library* tells you it is a place, it is at school, and people read there.

Look at the target words. Which words are new to you? Circle them here and in the reading.

Target Words

courses (paragraph 1)	**desk** (2)	**pair** (4)
education (1)	**famous** (3)	**busy** (5)
during (2)	**feelings** (3)	**misses** (5)
library (2)	**fingers** (4)	**dreams** (5)

Read "A Student and a Dancer" again. Look at the context of each new word. Can you guess the meaning?

Using the Vocabulary

A These sentences are **about the reading**. Complete them with the words in the box.

| busy | courses | during | ~~education~~ | famous | feelings | misses | pair |

1. People can study many things in college. Reyna wants to be a teacher, so she's studying ____education____.

2. Reyna is studying at a college. She's taking _____ at the college.

3. She has classes _____ the week but not on weekends.

4. People from many countries know about the flamenco. It's a _____ dance.

5. Reyna doesn't have much free time. She's usually _____ with schoolwork.

6. She doesn't often dance now, and she feels sad about that. She _____ dancing.

7. Flamenco music can make Reyna happy or sad. She shows her _____ in her dancing.

8. Reyna's hands move "like a _____ of flying birds" (like two flying birds).

B These sentences use the target words **in new contexts**. Complete them with the words in the box.

| busy | course | ~~during~~ | education | famous | feelings | misses | pair |

1. Please don't talk ____during____ the movie.

2. John wants to learn to speak Spanish, so he's taking a _____ in Spanish.

3. Everyone knows about Disney World. It's a very _____ place.

4. Do you want a good job? Then go to college and get a good _____.

5. That's a nice _____ of shoes.

6. Yuri is studying in the United States. His family and friends are back home in Russia. He thinks about them and he _____ them.

7. Maria is a student with a job and two small children. She has a

_____ life.

8. Is George happy? I don't know. He doesn't talk about his

_____.

 C Read these sentences. Match the **boldfaced** target words with their definitions.

a. She has beautiful hands with long **fingers**.

b. Do you remember your **dreams** in the morning?

c. Sometimes I go to the college **library**, and I sit at a **desk** to read and study.

Target Words   **Definitions**

1. ____library____ = a building with many books for people to use

2. _____ = a table you can sit at to write and work

3. _____ = things you think of in your sleep

4. _____ = the five long parts on your hand

Building on the Vocabulary

Studying Collocations

Collocations are words that we often put together. Some words can go together, and some can't. For example, we can say, I'm **taking** a math course. We can't say, I'm **making** a math course.

A Read these sentences with *take*. Complete the chart.

a taxi   *a camera*

1. We can **take a taxi** to the airport.
2. I **take the bus** to school.
3. Learning a language **takes time**.
4. The bus ride **takes an hour**.
5. You can **take pictures** with a camera.
6. Let's **take a walk** in the park.

	1. ____a taxi____
	2. _____
take +	3. _____
	4. _____
	5. _____
	6. _____

B Write four sentences. Use *take* + a word or phrase from the chart in Part A.

1. _____

2. _____

3. _____

4. _____

DEVELOPING YOUR SKILLS

Scanning

Sometimes you need to find a piece of information in a reading. To do this, you **scan** the reading. **Scan** means to read very quickly and look for just the information you need.

Where is the information about these topics in "A Student and a Dancer"? Scan the reading on page 3. Write the paragraph number (1–5).

_3_ **a.** flamenco music

_____ **b.** Reyna's dreams

_____ **c.** her future plans

_____ **d.** her hands

_____ **e.** her life every day

Summarizing

A **summary** tells a story again, but it has only the main information.

Some of the information in this summary of the reading is wrong. Find and correct six mistakes. The first mistake is corrected for you.

the United States

Reyna is a college student in ~~Venezuela~~. She plans to be a teacher, and

she's taking courses in math. She has to move a lot, and she doesn't like it. In

her free time, she plays the guitar. She says, "You have to feel the music in

your fingers." Every night, she dances in the library.

Discussion

Talk about these questions in a small group.

1. Reyna says she dreams about dancing. Do you remember your dreams?
2. Do you ever have dreams about dancing? about flying? about playing a guitar or another musical instrument? about doing something in the classroom?
3. What is a nice thing to dream about?

Using New Words

These questions use some of the target words. Ask and answer the questions with a partner. Then talk about your answers with the class.

1. Reyna **misses** dancing. What or who do you **miss**?
2. What **courses** are you taking this year?
3. What things do people buy in **pairs**?
4. Name three **famous** people. Why is each person **famous**?

Writing

Write sentences about your free time. Answer these questions.

1. When do you have free time?
2. What do you like to do in your free time?
3. Do you usually spend your free time alone or with other people?

Example:

1. I don't have much free time during the week. I have more free time on the weekend. I usually go out on Friday and Saturday nights.

CHAPTER 2

Making a Dream Come True

Tim and his plane

GETTING READY TO READ

Talk in a small group or with your class.

1. What do you see in the photo?
2. Do you like to fly? Why or why not?
3. Do you agree with these statements? Why or why not?
   - It's nice to spend your free time building something.
   - Building something takes a lot of hard work.

READING

Look at the words and pictures next to the reading. Then read.

Making a Dream Come True

1   Many houses in the United States have a driveway.[1] People often leave their cars in their driveways. But in the driveway at Tim Hoban's house, there's an airplane!

2   The plane is small—just about 20 feet long. (You can see the **size** of it in the photo on page 9.) It's not ready to fly **yet**. It has no **wings**, and there are no doors or windows on it. Parts of the plane are in boxes in the garage.[2] One box has pieces of the engine.[3] Tim Hoban is building this plane.

3   Building planes is not Tim's job. He works on the plane in his free time, in the evening and on weekends. **It takes time** to build a plane—a lot of time. "It's taking me hundreds of hours![4]" says Tim. "It's taking **too much** time!" says his wife. His **parents** smile and **shake their heads**. His friends laugh and tell him, "Tim, you're **crazy**!"

4   Tim is learning to fly at the airport near his home. A pilot[5] is teaching him. Tim can't fly alone yet. He needs to get a pilot's **license**. Soon Tim will take a **test** for his license. It won't be easy. The test will have two parts. Tim will take one part in a classroom. He'll answer questions about flying. For the second part, he'll fly a plane.

5   Tim is learning to fly in other people's planes, but he's **looking forward to** flying his **own** plane. He wants to get his plane out of the driveway and up into the air. He dreams about that day, and he keeps working.

[2] *a garage*

[1] *a driveway* →

[3] *an engine*

[4] *hundreds of hours* = more than 200 hours

[5] *a pilot* = a person who flies a plane

Quick Comprehension Check

Read these sentences. Circle T (true) or F (false).

1. Tim Hoban is building a small airplane at his home.   (T)   F

2. People in the United States often have planes in their driveways.   T   F

3. The plane is ready to fly now.   T   F

4. Tim is building his plane on weekends and after work.   T   F

5. Tim teaches courses in flying.   T   F

6. He will take a test to get a pilot's license.   T   F

EXPLORING VOCABULARY

Thinking about the Vocabulary

Look at the target words and phrases. Which are new to you? Circle them here and in the reading.

Target Words and Phrases		
size (2)	too much (3)	license (4)
yet (2)	parents (3)	test (4)
wings (2)	shake their heads (3)	looking forward to (5)
it takes time (3)	crazy (3)	own (5)

Read "Making a Dream Come True" again. Look at the context of each new word and phrase. Can you guess the meaning?

Using the Vocabulary

Ⓐ These sentences are **about the reading**. Complete them with the words and phrases in the box.

crazy	looking forward to	own	~~size~~	takes time	test	too much	yet

1. What _____size_____ is Tim's plane? It's about 20 feet long.

2. Tim needs to finish his plane. It can't fly now. It isn't ready

   _____ .

3. Tim says, "Building this plane is a lot of work. It _____, a lot of time."

4. Tim's wife is not happy. She says, "This plane is taking _____ time!"

5. Tim's friends say, "This plane is a bad idea, Tim. You're _____!"

6. Tim has to take a _____. It has questions about flying on it.

7. He wants to fly his _____ plane, not other people's planes.

8. Soon he'll fly his own plane. That idea makes him happy. He's _____ flying it.

B These sentences use the target words and phrases **in new contexts.**
Complete them with the words and phrases in the box.

crazy	look forward to	own	size	takes	~~tests~~	too much	yet

1. Anna is a very good math student. She usually gets 100% on math
   _____ tests _____.

2. Hiro wants to go to bed, but he has to do homework. He can't go to bed
   _____.

3. My sister wants to color her hair green. I think she's _____!

4. I live near school. I can walk to class, and it _____ me just five
   minutes.

5. I like these shoes, but they cost $400. That's _____ money for a
   pair of shoes.

6. Olga isn't happy. She and her sisters have one bedroom. She wants her
   _____ room.

7. I love weekends. All during the week, I _____ the weekend.

8. What _____ shoes do you wear? I wear an eight.

C **Label the pictures. Write** *a license, parents, shake your head,* **and** *a wing.*

mother   father

1. _____a wing_____

2. _____

3. _____

4. _____

Building on the Vocabulary

Studying Word Grammar

Nouns are words for:

people	*man, parents, Tim*
places	*airport, country, New York*
things	*plane, name, Toyota*
ideas	*education, love, time*

A **There are one or two nouns in each sentence. Circle the nouns.**

1. They are going to (Milton) by (car.)
2. The houses are small and white.
3. Do you like this music?
4. That woman is a famous dancer.
5. He is from Nigeria.
6. What size is this shirt?
7. Robert doesn't show his feelings.
8. The books are on my desk.

B Write sentences with these nouns: *test, parents, wings, license.*

1. _____

2. _____

3. _____

4. _____

DEVELOPING YOUR SKILLS

Scanning

Read these questions about "Making a Dream Come True." Scan the reading and write short answers.

1. How long is Tim's plane? _____ *about 20 feet* _____

2. What are the names of four parts of a plane? _____

3. When does Tim work on the plane? _____

4. Who says, "Tim, you're crazy!"? _____

5. What kind of license does Tim need to get? _____

6. How many parts will Tim's test have? _____

Thinking about the Main Idea

It's important to understand the **main idea** of a reading. The main idea is the most important information in the reading.

What is the main idea of "Making a Dream Come True"? Circle the answer.

1. Americans often build things like airplanes in their driveways.

2. Tim Hoban is working hard building a small plane and learning to fly.

3. Tim Hoban needs to get a pilot's license before he can fly.

Sharing Opinions

What do you think of these ideas? Check (✔) your opinions. Then talk about the ideas with a partner. Tell why you agree or disagree.

	Yes, I agree.	No, I disagree.
1. Building a plane at home is a crazy idea.		
2. Flying in a small plane seems like fun.		
3. When you build or make something, it's good to work alone. It's hard to do it with other people.		

Using New Words

Ask and answer these questions with a partner. Use one of the words or phrases in parentheses. Then talk about your answers with the class.

1. Do you have a (driver's/pilot's) **license**?
2. Do you have your **own** (room/car)?
3. What **size** (class/city) do you like most?
4. Do you have **too much** (money/free time)?
5. Do you **shake your head** when you (say "no"/think someone is crazy)?

Writing

What are you looking forward to in the future? Think of five things. Write five sentences with *I'm looking forward to*. You can use:

- *I'm looking forward to* + a noun:
  I'm looking forward to **the weekend**.

- *I'm looking forward to* + a verb ending in –*ing*:
  I'm looking forward to **seeing** my friends on Friday night.

CHAPTER 3

A Long-Distance Runner

Laura running in a race

GETTING READY TO READ

Talk with a partner or in a small group.

1. Look at the woman in the photo. What is she doing? How does she feel?
2. Make a list of things to do for exercise.
3. What do you like to do for exercise? What kinds of exercise do you *not* like?
4. How far can you run?

READING

Look at the words and pictures next to the reading. Then read.

A Long-Distance Runner

1   Lots of people like to run in their free time. Running is good **exercise**. Doctors say, "Getting exercise is important for good **health**." They suggest[1] thirty minutes of exercise three times a week.

2   Laura Gilbert usually runs three times a week. She sometimes runs alone and sometimes with friends. But thirty minutes of running isn't **enough** for her. Laura likes to run long **distances**. She says, "It takes me about forty minutes just to warm up.[2] I start feeling good after two hours." Each year, she runs **several** marathons. A marathon is 26.2 miles long (or 42.1 kilometers). Some of Laura's races[3] are **even** longer!

3   Every year, Laura runs in a race called *Il Passatore*. It's 101 kilometers long. That's more than 62 miles. The race begins near her home in Italy. The runners start in the city and run up into the **mountains**. They start at 3:00 P.M., and sometimes they run all night. The race takes Laura about twelve hours.

4   All year, Laura looks forward to Il Passatore. But before the race, she feels **nervous**. The race is a kind of test for her. Can she do it? During the race, her legs and feet and stomach[4] may **hurt**. She thinks about a hot bath. She thinks about her nice, soft bed. A part of her **mind** says, "Stop and go home! Why are you doing this? This is crazy!" But she **goes on** running. "I talk to other runners," she says, "and we help **each other**."

5   After 101 kilometers, Laura is **glad** to finish the race. Twelve hours are enough!

[1] *suggest* = say something is a good idea

[2] *warm up* = get ready to do something

[3] *race* = people doing something together to see who is the fastest

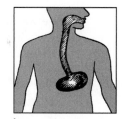

[4] the *stomach*

Quick Comprehension Check

Read these sentences. Circle T (true) or F (false).

1.	Laura Gilbert likes to run.	T	F
2.	She always runs alone.	T	F
3.	Laura thinks thirty minutes of running is too much.	T	F
4.	She runs in races of 26 miles and more.	T	F
5.	Before a big race, Laura feels happy.	T	F
6.	To Laura, a big race feels like a kind of test.	T	F

EXPLORING VOCABULARY

Thinking about the Vocabulary

Look at the target words and phrases. Which are new to you? Circle them here and in the reading.

Target Words and Phrases			
exercise (1)	several (2)	nervous (4)	goes on (4)
health (1)	even (2)	hurt (4)	each other (4)
enough (2)	mountains (3)	mind (4)	glad (5)
distances (2)			

Read "A Long-Distance Runner" again. Look at the context of each new word and phrase. Can you guess the meaning?

Using the Vocabulary

Ⓐ These sentences are about the reading. What is the meaning of each boldfaced word or phrase? Circle a, b, or c.

1. Laura likes to run for many miles. She likes to run long **distances**. *Distance* means:

   a. how often something happens   **b.** how far it is between two places   **c.** how tall something is

2. Getting **exercise** is good for us. It's good for our bodies. *Exercise* means:

   a. anything you do in your free time   **b.** moving your body to make it strong   **c.** running in long races

3. Marathons are long, but Il Passatore is **even** longer. *Even* is used to compare two things. It makes the second thing seem:

    a. the same as the first   b. not so important   c. greater or
                                                          more important

4. This race is like a test for Laura. It makes her feel **nervous**. *Nervous* means:

    a. afraid or worried   b. good or happy   c. great or
                                                   wonderful

5. During the race, the runners' legs sometimes **hurt**. *Hurt* means:

    a. feel bad   b. move   c. stop

6. Laura doesn't stop during the race. She **goes on** running. *Go on* means:

    a. wait   b. continue   c. leave

7. Laura and the other runners help **each other**. *Each other* shows that:

    a. each person helps   b. there are many   c. there is just
       the others   people in a group   one person

8. Laura is **glad** to talk to the other runners. *Glad* means:

    a. sorry   b. sad   c. happy

B These sentences use the target words and phrases **in new contexts.**
Complete them with the words in the box.

distances	each other	exercise	even	glad	go on	~~hurt~~	nervous

1. I have a problem with my teeth. They _____hurt_____. I need to see a
    dentist.

2. Sure, I can help you. No problem. I'll be _____ to help.

3. Jack sits and watches TV all the time. He doesn't get much

    _____.

4. Some bus drivers drive long _____ every day.

5. A cat is a small animal, but a mouse is _____ smaller.

6. Don't stop now! Please _____ and finish telling the story.

7. Paula and her sisters write letters to _____.

8. He's taking a test for his driver's license. He feels _____.

C Read these sentences. Match the **boldfaced** target words with their definitions.

a. Eat well for good **health**.

b. Do you want Chinese food tonight? I know **several** good Chinese restaurants.

c. He has many things to think about. He has a lot on his **mind**.

d. The Himalayas, the Andes, and the Alps are famous **mountains**.

e. I like a little sugar in my coffee—not too much. A little sugar is **enough** for me.

Target Words	Definitions

1. __mountains__ = very high hills

2. _____ = more than two but not many

3. _____ = as much as you need; the right amount

4. _____ = a person's thoughts and ideas

5. _____ = how well you feel

Building on the Vocabulary

Studying Collocations

Remember: Collocations are words that we use together. Some words can go together, and some cannot. For example, *get* goes with *exercise*. We can say, *Let's **get** some exercise.* We cannot say, *Let's **take** some exercise.*

A Complete these sentences with *get* or *take*.

1. A person has to _____get_____ a license to fly a plane.

2. The students have to _____ a test on Friday.

3. I usually _____ some exercise on weekends.

4. The homework is hard. It's going to _____ me a long time.

5. It's important to _____ a good education.

6. I'm planning to _____ a math course.

B Write four sentences with *get* or *take* + *a license, a test, an education, some exercise, a course,* or *a long time.*

1. _____

2. _____

3. _____

4. _____

DEVELOPING YOUR SKILLS

Understanding Sentences with *Because*

Sentences with *because* answer the question *Why?*

Choose the best way to complete each sentence.

___c___ 1. Doctors tell us to get exercise

_____ 2. Laura Gilbert runs

_____ 3. Il Passatore takes Laura about twelve hours

_____ 4. Laura feels nervous before the race

_____ 5. Runners sometimes talk to each other

a. because it's 101 kilometers long.

b. because it can be hard to run alone.

c. because it's good for our health.

d. because running feels good to her.

e. because it feels like a test to her.

Summarizing

Some of the information in this summary of the reading is wrong. Find and correct six mistakes. The first mistake is corrected for you.

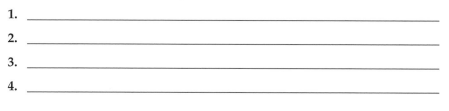

Laura Gilbert likes to run ~~short~~ distances. She starts to feel good after

running for two miles. Every week, she runs a 101-kilometer race called Il

Passatore. She runs it near her home in Italy. Her legs and her feet sometimes

break during the race. The runners in this race hurt each other. Laura always

feels crazy after this race.

Discussion

Talk about these questions in a small group.

1. When and why does Laura feel nervous?

2. When do you feel nervous? Check (✔) your answers.

   I feel nervous when . . .

   ❏ I take a test in school.   ❏ I meet someone new.

   ❏ I go to the doctor.   ❏ I talk to a big group of people.

   ❏ I'm in the dentist's chair.   ❏ _____

3. Do you think long-distance runners are crazy? Why or why not?

Using New Words

Ask and answer these questions with a partner. Use one of the words or phrases in parentheses. Then talk about questions 3 and 4 with the class.

1. Are you in (good/bad) **health**?

2. How can you complete this statement? In my (bag/pocket/home), I have **several** . . .

3. How much (homework/TV/exercise) is **enough** for one day? How much is too much?

4. How can students help **each other**?

Writing

Complete the answers to these questions. Then use your answers to write a paragraph.

• When do you feel nervous?

  I feel nervous when _____.

• What happens to you when you are nervous? Do you feel changes in your body or your mind?

  When I am nervous, _____.

• What do you do to feel better?

  I _____, and then I feel better.

Example:

   I feel nervous when I speak in front of the class. When I am nervous, sometimes my hands shake and my face feels hot. I forget things to say. I look at my friends in the class, and they smile at me. They want to help me. I sit down, and then I feel better.

CHAPTER 4

Playing with Words

Ferdie at work

Ferdie at home

GETTING READY TO READ

Talk in a small group or with your class.

1. What do you see in the photos?
2. Do you ever play board games[1]?
3. How can playing games help you learn English?
4. How many of you know the game Scrabble?®

[1] Checkers, chess, and Scrabble are *board games.*

READING

Look at the words and picture next to the reading. Then read.

Playing with Words

1   Ferdie Adoboe's work is like some people's play. What does he do?[1] He plays on a soccer[2] **team**, and he teaches the game of soccer. In his free time, he likes to play a very different game. He likes to exercise his mind with the game of Scrabble.

2   Do you know Scrabble? It's a game of words. It's famous in many countries. You can buy Scrabble in twenty-three languages. Each person in the game has seven letters. Players use their letters to **spell** words and get points.[3] For example, you get one point for the letters *L, I,* or *E.* The letter *K* **is worth** five points. So you can get eight points for the word *like.*

3   Ferdie says, "It's not hard to learn Scrabble. It's **simple**! People can **have fun** and work on their English at the same time." English is not Ferdie's first language. He's from Ghana, in West Africa, and his family speaks Fanti. English is important in Ghana, **especially** for a good education.

4   Now Ferdie lives and works in the United States. He teaches soccer to young people all over the country. He teaches in other countries, too, so Ferdie **travels** a lot. He takes a **tiny** Scrabble game with him on the plane. Sometimes he plays Scrabble with other soccer players.

5   At home, Ferdie is teaching his daughters to play his **favorite** game. Sometimes he plays Scrabble online.[4] He also **invites** friends to his house, and they play together. Sometimes their games take several hours.

6   Here is **another** interesting **fact** about Ferdie: You can **look up** his name in the *Guinness Book of World Records.* He's a very fast runner, and he holds the world **record** for running backwards![5]

[1] *What does he do?* = What is his job?

[2] *soccer* See the photo on page 23

[3] *points* = the numbers you win in a game

[4] *online* = using a computer and the Internet

[5] *running backwards*

Quick Comprehension Check

Read these sentences. Circle T (true) or F (false).

1. Ferdie Adoboe is a soccer player.   T   F

2. He plays Scrabble in his free time.   T   F

3. Scrabble is a game of words.   T   F

4. It's a game for one person to play alone.   T   F

5. Ferdie is on a Scrabble team, and he teaches Scrabble
   in other countries.   T   F

6. Ferdie can run very fast.   T   F

EXPLORING VOCABULARY

Thinking about the Vocabulary

Look at the target words and phrases. Which are new to you? Circle them here and in the reading.

Target Words and Phrases				
team (1)	simple (3)	travels (4)	invites (5)	look up (6)
spell (2)	have fun (3)	tiny (4)	another (6)	record (6)
is worth (2)	especially (3)	favorite (5)	fact (6)	

Read "Playing with Words" again. Look at the context of each new word and phrase. Can you guess the meaning?

Using the Vocabulary

Ⓐ These sentences are about the reading. Complete them with the words and phrases in the box.

especially	have fun	invites	is worth	look up	record	~~spell~~	travels

1. Scrabble players put letters together and _____spell_____ words.

2. Each letter _____ points. For example, you win five points for using the letter *K*.

3. Many people like to play Scrabble. They _____ with this game.

4. English is important in Ghana. It's _____ important in the schools.

5. Ferdie doesn't stay at home. He _____ all over the world.

6. Ferdie calls his friends and _____ them to come to his house.

7. Open the *Guinness Book of World Records*, and _____ Ferdie's name. You will find it there.

8. Ferdie holds the world _____ for running backwards. He's very, very fast. He's number one in the world.

B These sentences use the target words and phrases **in new contexts**. Complete them with the words and phrases in the box.

| especially | have fun | invite | is worth | look up | record | spell | ~~travel~~ |

1. My parents don't like airplanes. They always _____travel_____ by car.

2. We'd like to _____ you to our house for dinner. How about Friday?

3. I don't know her phone number. I need to _____ her number in the phone book.

4. Today is our twenty-fifth day of rain! It's a new _____.

5. John loves ice cream, _____ chocolate ice cream.

6. How does she _____ her name? Is it *A-n-n* or *A-n-n-e*?

7. I'm going to sell my car. I'm going to ask $2,000 for it. I think it _____ $2,000.

8. You'll like college. You'll meet new friends and _____ with them.

C Read each **definition** and look at the paragraph number. Look back at the reading to find the target word for each definition. Complete the chart.

DEFINITION	PARAGRAPH	TARGET WORD
1. a group of people who play and work together	1	____team____
2. easy to do or understand	3	_____
3. very, very small	4	_____
4. liked more than others	5	_____
5. one more	6	_____
6. a piece of true information	6	_____

Building on the Vocabulary

Studying Word Grammar

Verbs are words for actions (for example, *run*, *fly*, *dance*, and *play*). The words *have* and *be* are also verbs. Some verbs are more than one word (for example, *go on* and *warm up*).

A Circle the verb in each sentence.

1. He (is) on a good team.
2. My head hurts.
3. They are fast runners.
4. She is shaking her head.
5. I have fun on the weekend.
6. She misses her family.
7. Think about your health.
8. He gets a lot of exercise.

B Write sentences with these verbs: *travel, invite, look up, spell.*

1. _____
2. _____
3. _____
4. _____

DEVELOPING YOUR SKILLS

Scanning

**Where is the information about these topics in "Playing with Words"?
Scan the reading on page 24. Write the paragraph number (1–6).**

   _5_   **a.** Ferdie's children
   _____ **b.** languages in Ghana
   _____ **c.** Ferdie's world record
   _____ **d.** why he travels a lot
   _____ **e.** how to play Scrabble
   _____ **f.** Ferdie's last name

Thinking about the Main Idea

What is the main idea of "Playing with Words"? Circle the answer.

1. You can play soccer and work on your English at the same time.
2. Ferdie Adoboe loves two games: soccer and Scrabble.
3. Scrabble is a game of words, and it's easy to learn.

Interviewing

Read the questions in the chart. Write your answers. Then interview a partner. Write your partner's answers.

	YOU	YOUR PARTNER
1. What languages do people use in your country?		
2. Is English important in your country? If you say *Yes*, who uses English?		
3. Why are you learning English?		

Using New Words

Ask and answer these questions with a partner. Then talk about questions 2, 3, and 4 with the class.

1. How do you **spell** your first name?
2. What things are **simple** to cook or make? Make a list.
3. What things are **tiny**? Make a list.
4. Brazil has good soccer **teams**. What's **another** country with good soccer **teams**?

Writing

Choose sentence 1, 2, or 3. Complete it, and add two more sentences about the topic to make a paragraph.

1. My favorite team is _____.
2. I like to play _____, especially _____.
3. Sometimes I invite a friend to _____.

Example:

My favorite team is the Yomiuri Giants. They are a baseball team in my city, Tokyo. I watch them on TV, and I sometimes go to their games with my friends.

Wrap-up

REVIEWING VOCABULARY

A Complete these sentences with the words and phrases below. Two words do not belong in the sentences.

during	each other	enough	especially	even
health	hurt	~~pair~~	too much	yet

1. I need a new _____pair_____ of sunglasses.

2. Those two people love _____.

3. China is big, but Russia is _____ bigger.

4. He can't buy a new car. He doesn't have _____ money.

5. Most students have very busy lives, _____ on school days.

6. The doctor isn't here _____, but she'll be here soon.

7. Exercise, good food, and enough sleep are important for good

   _____.

8. I can't hear you. There's _____ noise here. Let's go somewhere quiet.

B Match the words and phrases with their definitions. There are two extra words in the box.

desk	favorite	fingers	go on	invite
look up	size	~~spell~~	team	wings

1. _____spell_____ = tell the letters in a word

2. _____ = people working or playing as a group

3. _____ = continue, keep doing something

4. _____ = try to find some information (in a phone book, at the library, etc.)

5. _____ = how big or how small something is

6. _____ = parts of a bird or a plane that help it fly

7. _____ = a kind of table that you sit at to study or write

8. _____ = ask someone to do something with you

29

EXPANDING VOCABULARY

A Some words can be nouns or verbs. Remember: A noun is a word for a person, place, thing, or idea. A verb is a word for an action.

Look at the boldfaced words in these sentences. Write *noun* or *verb* after each word.

1. a. How much **sleep** do you need? _____noun_____

   b. I **sleep** late on Sundays. Do you? _____

2. a. **Exercise** is good for your health. _____

   b. Where do you usually **exercise**? Do you have a favorite place? _____

3. a. The teacher will **test** us on the new words from this unit. _____

   b. The **test** will be next Friday. _____

4. a. Do you remember your **dreams**? _____

   b. Do you sometimes **dream** about school? _____

5. a. Yoko often **travels** to other countries. _____

   b. She writes me letters about her **travels**. _____

6. a. I'm **feeling** sick. My stomach hurts. _____

   b. I have a strange **feeling** in my stomach. _____

B Certain verbs and nouns form collocations. Remember: collocations are words that often go together. For example, we can say, *All drivers need to **take** a test,* but we cannot say, *All drivers need to **do** a test* or *All drivers need to **make** a test.*

Complete the collocations. Write the noun that goes with each verb.

Nouns:

a course
an education
fun
a record

1. get _____

2. have _____

3. take _____

4. hold _____

PLAYING WITH WORDS

Complete the sentences with words you studied in Chapters 1–4. Write the words in the puzzle.

Across

2. What's the distance_____ from the earth to the sun?

4. Everybody knows his name. He's f_____.

9. Look at the baby's little fingers. They're t_____!

10. That m_____ is 14,000 feet high.

11. Two pizzas won't be enough. We'll need s_____ of them.

12. My friends aren't here with me. I m_____ them.

Down

1. You can take books home from the l_____.

3. Don't do that! It's c_____!

5. Do you want to use my book, or do you have your o_____ book?

6. It's not hard at all. It's s_____.

7. She has many things to think about. She has too much on her m_____.

8. That book is full of f_____ about airplanes.

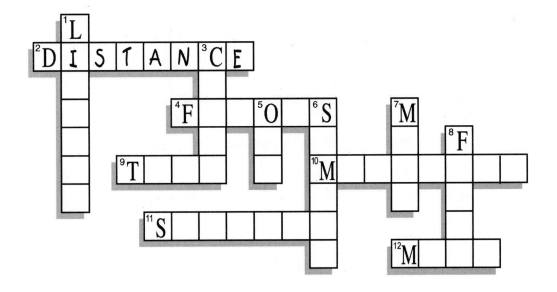

BUILDING DICTIONARY SKILLS

Guidewords help you find words in the dictionary. Look at these pages. The guidewords are *before* and *below*. *Before* is the first word on the left page; *below* is the last word on the right page.

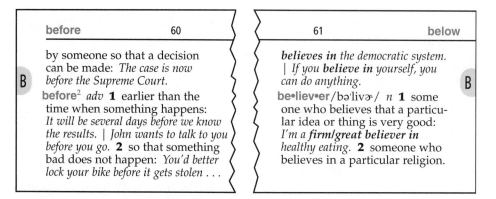

| before | 60 |

B

by someone so that a decision can be made: *The case is now before the Supreme Court.*
before² *adv* **1** earlier than the time when something happens: *It will be several days before we know the results.* | *John wants to talk to you before you go.* **2** so that something bad does not happen: *You'd better lock your bike before it gets stolen . . .*

| 61 | below |

B

believes in the democratic system. | *If you **believe in** yourself, you can do anything.*
be•liev•er /bəˈlivɚ/ *n* **1** someone who believes that a particular idea or thing is very good: *I'm a **firm/great believer in** healthy eating.* **2** someone who believes in a particular religion.

Ⓐ **Will these words be on pages 60–61? Check *Yes* or *No*.**

	YES	NO
1. blue		✔
2. begin		
3. belong		
4. beeper		
5. believe		
6. bilingual		

Ⓑ **Write the words from Part A in alphabetical order.**

1. _beeper_   4. _____

2. _____   5. _____

3. _____   6. _____

UNIT 2

PLACES AROUND THE WORLD

CHAPTER 5

Antarctica

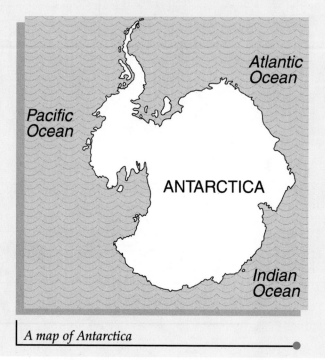

A map of Antarctica

GETTING READY TO READ

Talk with a partner about these statements. Do you think they are true or false? Circle your answers.

1. Antarctica is the same size as Australia.   T   F

2. Antarctica has 50% of the world's fresh water.[1]   T   F

3. It is summer now in Antarctica.   T   F

4. There are volcanoes[2] in Antarctica.   T   F

5. No one lives in Antarctica.   T   F

6. Some people visit Antarctica just for fun.   T   F

[1] *fresh water =* water without salt, as in lakes or rivers

[2] a *volcano*

READING

Look at the words and pictures next to the reading. Then read without stopping. Don't worry about new words. Don't stop to use a dictionary. Just keep reading!

Antarctica

1   Antarctica is one of the seven **continents**[1]. Can you name the others? They are Africa, Asia, Australia, Europe, North America, and South America. All six of these continents are home to many important people, places, and things. But what about Antarctica?

2   Some people think Antarctica is just an **empty** place. They say, "There's nothing there—just **ice** and **snow**." But Antarctica is an important part of the world. For one thing,[2] about 70%[3] of the world's fresh water is there.

3   Antarctica is not the smallest continent. It's bigger than Australia, and it's bigger than Europe. It's almost as **large** as[4] South America. There are three oceans around Antarctica. Look at the **map** on page 34 and read their names in English: the Atlantic, the Pacific, and the Indian Oceans. They all **touch** part of Antarctica.

4   **Of course** you know this fact about Antarctica: It's *cold!* It has about 90% of the ice in the world! In the winter, the sun doesn't **shine** for several months. Then the **temperature** of the air can go **below** -110° F (-80° C).[5] In the summer, the sun shines almost all the time, but it's never really warm.

5   Penguins[6] live in Antarctica, but people don't. **However**, every year, several thousand people stay and work there. They stay for weeks or even months. Most of these people are **scientists**. They come from many different countries. They come to study changes in the weather and learn about living things in the ocean. They also study the water, the air, and the **land**. They even study volcanoes there!

6   A few people travel to Antarctica just for fun. They say it's a beautiful place. What do you think of that idea? Would you like[7] to visit Antarctica?

---

[1] **Continents by Size**

1	Asia
2	Africa
3	North America
4	South America
5	Antarctica
6	Europe
7	Australia

[2] *for one thing =* here is one example or reason

[3] *% = percent*

[4] *as large as =* the same size as

[5] *-110° F (-80° C) =* "minus . . . degrees Fahrenheit/Celsius"

[6] *a penguin*

[7] *would you like =* do you want

Quick Comprehension Check

Ⓐ Read these sentences. Circle T (true) or F (false).

1.	Antarctica is a country.	T	F
2.	Most of the world's fresh water is in Antarctica.	T	F
3.	Antarctica is smaller than Australia or Europe.	T	F
4.	There are three oceans next to Antarctica.	T	F
5.	Penguins live in Antarctica.	T	F
6.	Scientists from many countries go to Antarctica to work.	T	F

Ⓑ Look back at the true/false statements on page 34. Check your answers.

EXPLORING VOCABULARY

Thinking about the Vocabulary

Which target words and phrases are new to you? Circle them here and in the reading. Then read "Antarctica" again. Look at the context of each new word and phrase. Can you guess the meaning?

Target Words and Phrases			
continents (1)	large (3)	shine (4)	scientists (5)
empty (2)	map (3)	temperature (4)	land (5)
ice (2)	touch (3)	below (4)	
snow (2)	of course (4)	however (5)	

Using the Vocabulary

Ⓐ These sentences are **about the reading**. Complete them with the target words and phrases in the box.

below	however	~~ice~~	of course	shines	snow	temperature	touches

1. It is very, very cold in Antarctica, so water changes into _____ice_____ .
2. In Antarctica, the sun _____ for weeks in the summer. It doesn't go down at night.

3. The weather never gets warm in Antarctica. The _____ never goes very high.

4. There isn't much rain in Antarctica, but there's a lot of _____.

5. _____ you know it's cold in Antarctica. Everybody knows that!

6. People don't live in Antarctica. _____ , scientists stay there for weeks or even months.

7. The temperature in Antarctica is usually _____ 32° F (0° C). It doesn't usually go above 32° F (0° C).

8. The Pacific Ocean _____ part of Antarctica. The Atlantic and Indian Oceans do, too.

B These sentences use the target words and phrases **in new contexts.**
Complete them with the words and phrases in the box.

below	however	ice	of course	shine	snow	~~temperature~~	touch

1. I'm sick. I feel hot. I'm going to take my __temperature__ .

2. Is your drink cold enough? Would you like some _____ in your glass?

3. In places with cold winters, children have fun in the _____.

4. I don't like cold weather; _____, I love snow. It's beautiful!

5. Can I spell *cat?* Yes, _____ I can! It's simple: c-a-t.

6. At night, lights _____ from the windows of people's homes.

7. Be careful! Don't _____ that! It's very hot.

8. Our apartment is on the third floor. They live _____ us on the second floor.

C Read these sentences. Match the **boldfaced** target words with their definitions.

a. China is a **large** country in Asia. Asia is the largest **continent** in the world.

b. Where are you from? Please show me on this **map**.

c. Dr. Smith is a **scientist**. He studies the sun and other stars.

d. She has nothing to drink. Her glass is **empty**.

e. Penguins spend a lot of time in the water, but they live on **land**.

Target Words	Definitions
1. ____large____	= big
2. _____	= having nothing inside
3. _____	= the part of the earth that is not under water
4. _____	= one of seven large areas of land in the world
5. _____	= a person who studies things in the natural world
6. _____	= a picture showing where things are in a city, a country, or another place

Building on the Vocabulary

Studying Word Grammar

An **adjective** is a word that describes a person, place, or thing. The words *hot*, *red*, and *beautiful* are adjectives.
- Adjectives can come before nouns: *I have* **good friends**.
- Adjectives can come after the verb *be*: *John and Mary* **are happy**.

 A **There are one or two adjectives in each sentence. Circle the adjectives.**

1. She's a (busy) woman.
2. He's tall and handsome.
3. The men are famous actors.
4. We're enjoying nice, warm weather.
5. They're nervous about flying.
6. I'll be glad to help.

B **Write sentences with these adjectives:** *empty, large, crazy, favorite.*

1. _____
2. _____
3. _____
4. _____

DEVELOPING YOUR SKILLS

Scanning

Read these questions about "Antarctica." Scan the reading, and write short answers.

1. What is Antarctica? _____ *a continent* _____

2. What are the other six continents? _____

   _____

3. How much of the world's fresh water is in Antarctica? _____%

4. How much of the ice in the world is in Antarctica? _____%

5. What happens to the air temperature in the winter? _____

   _____

6. How many people work in Antarctica? _____

7. What do they study? _____

Thinking about the Main Idea

What is the main idea of "Antarctica"? Circle the answer.

1. Antarctica has most of the world's fresh water.

2. Everyone should visit Antarctica.

3. Antarctica is an interesting and important part of the world.

Discussion

Talk about these questions in a small group.

1. In the future, ships might pull large pieces of ice from Antarctica across the ocean. They would take the ice to countries that need fresh water. What do you think of this idea? Which countries might want to do this?

2. Some people visit Antarctica just for fun. Would you like to go there? Why or why not?

Using New Words

Work with a partner. Choose five target words or phrases from the list on page 36. On a piece of paper, use each word or phrase in a sentence.

Writing

Where in the world do you want to go? Choose a place to visit and write a paragraph about it. Give three or more facts about the place. Answer these questions:

- Where is it?
- What can you see and do there?
- What's the weather like?
- Why do you want to go there?

  You can begin with: *I would like to visit . . .*

CHAPTER 6

The Galápagos

A tortoise on the beach in the Galápagos

A map of the Galápagos Islands

GETTING READY TO READ

Talk with a partner or in a small group.

1. Can you label the pictures of these animals? Write *a penguin, an iguana,* or *a sea lion* under each picture.

a. _____   b. _____   c. _____

2. What kinds of animals do you like to touch? What kinds do you not like to touch?

3. What is a good place to see interesting animals?

READING

Look at the words and pictures next to the reading. Then read.

The Galápagos

1 There is an **unusual** group of **islands** in the Pacific Ocean about 600 miles to the **west** of South America. They are near the equator.[1] These islands are part of Ecuador, a small country in South America. In English, they are called the Galápagos.

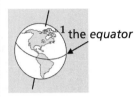

[1] the *equator*

2 The Galápagos are famous because of their animals. Their animals are unusual in two ways. First, some of them live in just this one part of the world. You can't find them anywhere **else**. For example, there are some very big tortoises here. (*Galápago* is a Spanish word for *tortoise*.) Second, the animals are not afraid of people. Visitors can sit down next to iguanas on the **rocks**. They can walk very close to sea lions on the **beach**. They can even swim with them in the ocean!

3 Do you like to watch birds? There are more than eighty different kinds of birds here, even one kind of penguin. Penguins usually live in cold places, so finding them near the equator seems strange. However, cold water travels **north**[2] from Antarctica **along** South America. It brings down the temperature of the water around the Galápagos. It makes the water **cool** enough for penguins.

[2]

4 There are a lot of very small islands in the Galápagos. Thirteen of the islands are larger. People live on five of these, but most of the land in the Galápagos is just for animals. Some of these animals, **such as** the tortoises, **belong to** endangered species.[3] In the Galápagos, no one will hurt them. The people of Ecuador want to **protect** these animals. Their **government** will go on working to keep the animals **safe**.

[3] *endangered species* = kinds of animals that soon might not exist

Quick Comprehension Check

Read these sentences. Circle T (true) or F (false).

1.	The Galápagos are a group of islands.	T	F
2.	These islands are part of Ecuador.	T	F
3.	They are famous because of their beautiful beaches.	T	F
4.	Some unusual animals live in the Galápagos.	T	F
5.	People can't go near the animals.	T	F
6.	People don't live on most of the islands; just animals do.	T	F

EXPLORING VOCABULARY

Thinking about the Vocabulary

Which target words and phrases are new to you? Circle them here and in the reading. Then read "The Galápagos" again. Look at the context of each new word and phrase. Can you guess the meaning?

Target Words and Phrases			
unusual (1)	**rocks** (2)	**cool** (3)	**government** (4)
islands (1)	**beach** (2)	**such as** (4)	**safe** (4)
west (1)	**north** (3)	**belong to** (4)	
else (2)	**along** (3)	**protect** (4)	

Using the Vocabulary

Ⓐ **Label these pictures. Write *beach*, *cool*, *island*, and *rock*.**

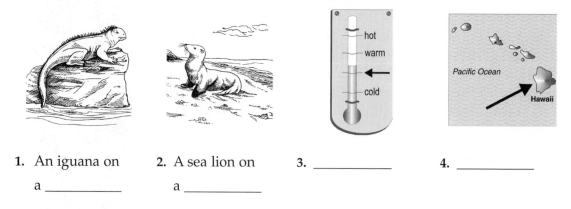

1. An iguana on a _____	2. A sea lion on a _____	3. _____	4. _____

B These sentences are **about the reading.** Complete them with the words and phrases in the box.

along	belong to	else	government	north
protect	safe	such as	unusual	~~west~~

1. The Galápagos are islands in the Pacific to the _____west_____ of South America.

2. The Galápagos are different from most other islands. They are

   _____.

3. The tortoises of the Galápagos live in this one place, not anywhere

   _____.

4. Cold water from Antarctica moves _____ and comes to the Galápagos.

5. The cold water travels north by the side of South America. It travels _____ the beaches of South America.

6. The tortoises on the Galápagos are part of a larger group. This group is a species. The tortoises _____ an endangered species.

7. Several kinds of animals, _____ the tortoise, live here. (The tortoise is an example.)

8. In the Galápagos, no one hurts the animals. They have a _____ home there.

9. The people of Ecuador want to keep these animals safe. They want to _____ them.

10. The _____ of Ecuador is trying to protect the animals of the Galápagos.

C These sentences use the target words and phrases **in new contexts.** Complete them with the words and phrases in the box.

along	~~belong to~~	else	government	north
protect	safe	such as	unusual	west

1. About 200 countries _____belong to_____ the United Nations.

2. Elephants live in Africa and India. Do they live anywhere _____?

3. I like to walk _____ the river and watch the boats.

4. Most birds can fly. However, penguins can't. They are _____ birds.

5. Please don't ride your bike at night. You don't have a light, so it's not

_____ .

6. Workers sometimes wear safety glasses to _____ their eyes.

7. Who leads the _____ in your country? Is there a president?

8. Some colors, _____ light blue or green, are called *cool colors*.

9. The sun goes down in the _____ .

10. In the United States, birds fly _____ in the spring.

Building on the Vocabulary

Studying Collocations

The phrase **anywhere else** is used in the reading on page 41. *Else* means *different* or *other*. *Else* is often used with words like *anybody*, *something*, and *everyone*.

 **Read the sentences below. Underline the word before *else*.**

1. Our teacher won't be here tomorrow. <u>Someone</u> **else** will teach our class.

2. I'm going to get some coffee. Would anyone **else** like some?

3. The little boy wants ice cream. Nothing **else** will make him happy.

4. What should we buy for her birthday, a CD? I can't think of anything **else**.

5. That part of the library is closed, but you can go everywhere **else** in the building.

6. This store doesn't have good clothes. Let's go somewhere **else**.

B **Complete these phrases. Use the words from Part A.**

1. ___someone___ + else = some other person

2. _____ + else = any other person

3. _____ + else = no other thing

4. _____ + else = any other thing

5. _____ + else = every other place

6. _____ + else = some other place

C **Complete these sentences. Use the phrases with *else* from Part B.**

1. I know Marta, but I don't know ___anyone else___ in that class.

2. He's crazy about cars. He talks about cars all the time. He talks about

   _____!

3. She doesn't live at her parents' house now. She lives _____.

4. We have to clean our apartment. The kitchen is okay, but we have to clean

   _____.

5. I'm going to the store for some bread. Do we need _____?

6. I'm sorry, but I don't know the time. I don't have a watch. Ask

   _____.

DEVELOPING YOUR SKILLS

Pronoun Reference

A **pronoun** (*such as he, she, it,* or *them*) takes the place of a noun. A pronoun usually comes after a noun and it refers back to the noun. We often use a pronoun so that a noun is not repeated.

What do the boldfaced pronouns mean in these sentences? Look back at the reading.

1. Paragraph 1: In English, **they** are called the Galápagos.   ___the islands___

2. Paragraph 2: You can't find **them** anywhere else.   _____

3. Paragraph 2: **They** can walk very close to sea lions.   _____

4. Paragraph 3: **It** brings down the temperature of the water.   _____

5. Paragraph 4: In the Galápagos, no one will hurt **them**.   _____

Summarizing

Some of the information in this summary of the reading is wrong. Find and correct six mistakes. The first mistake is corrected for you.

islands

The Galápagos are ~~countries~~ to the west of South America. They are near

the equator, but the ocean water is hot. The Galápagos are famous because of

their beaches. The animals are not afraid of each other. Some of these animals,

but not the tortoises, belong to endangered species. The Ecuadorian

government is working to kill them.

Categorizing

A **category** is a group of people or things of the same kind. The people or things in a category are like each other in some way.

Ⓐ Work with a partner. Name each of these categories.

1. Ecuador, Korea, Canada, Turkey, Russia   _____countries_____

2. red, green, blue, black, yellow   _____

3. Antarctica, Asia, South America, Europe, Africa   _____

4. coffee, tea, juice, water, milk   _____

5. soccer, swimming, tennis, basketball, baseball   _____

6. parents, students, scientists, visitors, doctors   _____

7. tortoises, penguins, sea lions, iguanas   _____

Ⓑ With your partner, think of another category. List five people or things that belong in this category.

Category: _____ _____

_____

Using New Words

Ask and answer these questions with a partner. Talk about your answers with the class.

1. Can you name three **islands**? Tell where they are.
2. What country is to the **north** of your country? What country is to the **west**?
3. Does your country **belong to** the United Nations?
4. Where do you feel **safe**? Where do you not feel **safe**?

Writing

Choose sentence 1, 2, or 3. Complete it, and add two or more sentences about the topic.

1. I (would like/wouldn't like) to visit the Galápagos because . . .
2. A good beach . . .
3. A _____ is a good pet because . . .
   _(a kind of animal)

Example:

A good beach has nice, white sand. The water is clean and not very cold. There are big waves, but you can swim. There are not a lot of people and no loud radios. You can go to sleep.

CHAPTER 7

San Marino

Mount Titano in San Marino

A tiny country

GETTING READY TO READ

Talk with a partner or in a small group.

1. What continent is San Marino on?
2. What do you think comes from San Marino? Circle your answers.

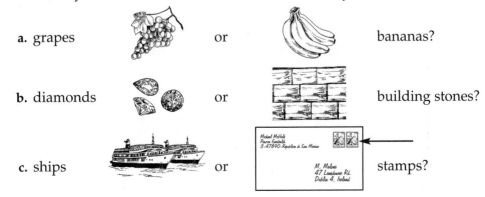

   a. grapes   or   bananas?

   b. diamonds   or   building stones?

   c. ships   or   stamps?

READING

Look at the words and pictures next to the reading. Then read.

San Marino

1   Close your eyes and **imagine** this: You are a visitor to San Marino. It's a beautiful warm day in May. This afternoon, you have some free time. Would you like to take a walk? In one afternoon, a person can walk across the **whole** country!

2   San Marino is very small—**only** 23 square miles.[1] From **east** to west, it's no more than 6 miles (9 kilometers). It's smaller than many cities.

3   What will you see and hear on your walk? Let's begin at the border[2] between San Marino and Italy. (Italy is San Marino's only **neighbor**. San Marino is **completely** inside it.) You can see **farms** on much of the land around you. Some of San Marino's farm **products** are wheat,[3] olives,[4] and grapes. About two miles away, in the center of the country, you can see a mountain. That's Mount Titano. There are nine small towns on the mountain. In these towns, you'll see old **stone** buildings with red **roofs**.

4   All around you, you'll hear people speaking Italian. Maybe you'll hear other languages, such as Spanish, German, French, and Japanese. Why? You are not the only visitor to San Marino today. This little country has more than three million visitors each year. No one really knows the number. The government doesn't stop visitors at the border to **count** them. People come and go freely here.

5   Why do so many visitors come to San Marino? Some people come to learn about its **history**. They want to see the old buildings and **find out** about the past. Others come to buy coins[5] and stamps. People all over the world **collect** the beautiful and unusual stamps of San Marino.

6   Are you **getting** tired from your walk? Then it's time to sit down and have a nice, cool drink or a *gelato*—an Italian ice cream. Enjoy!

[1] a *square mile*

[2] *border* = the line between two countries

[3] *wheat*

[4] *olives*

[5] *coins*

Quick Comprehension Check

A Read these sentences. Circle T (true) or F (false).

1.	San Marino is a city in Italy.	T	F
2.	From east to west, San Marino is only a few miles across.	T	F
3.	Bananas are an important farm product in this country.	T	F
4.	Many visitors come to San Marino.	T	F
5.	The government stops all visitors coming into the country.	T	F
6.	Visitors can buy beautiful and unusual stamps and coins.	T	F

B Look back at the questions on page 47. Check your answers.

EXPLORING VOCABULARY

Thinking about the Vocabulary

Which target words and phrases are new to you? Circle them here and in the reading. Then read "San Marino" again. Look at the context of each new word and phrase. Can you guess the meaning?

Target Words and Phrases		
imagine (1)	completely (3)	count (4)
whole (1)	farms (3)	history (5)
only (2)	products (3)	find out (5)
east (2)	stone (3)	collect (5)
neighbor (3)	roofs (3)	getting (6)

Using the Vocabulary

A These sentences are about the reading. What is the meaning of each **boldfaced** word or phrase? Circle a, b, or c.

1. **Imagine** that you are in San Marino. You aren't really there. *Imagine* means:

   a. make a picture in your mind
   b. be glad
   c. decide or believe

2. San Marino is **only** a few miles across. *Only* means:

   a. usually
   b. right now
   c. just

3. San Marino is **completely** inside Italy. *Completely* means:

   a. maybe   **b.** totally   **c.** now

4. People can walk across the **whole** country of San Marino. The whole something is:

   a. half of it   **b.** most of it   **c.** all of it

5. Many buildings in San Marino are made of **stone**. *Stone* means:

   a. rock   **b.** ice   **c.** snow

6. Grapes, olives, and stamps are some of the **products** of San Marino. Products are:

   a. things people make or grow to sell   **b.** things people like to keep   **c.** things people eat or drink

7. From a plane, you can see the red **roofs** of San Marino. A roof is _____ of a building.

   a. the front   **b.** the top   **c.** the inside

8. Some visitors come to **find out** about San Marino's history. *Find out* means:

   a. teach   **b.** dream   **c.** learn

9. Would you like to rest? Are you **getting** tired? *Getting* in this sentence means:

   a. taking   **b.** becoming   **c.** buying

B These sentences use the target words and phrases **in new contexts.** Complete them with the words in the box.

~~completely~~	find out	get	imagine	only
products	roof	stone	whole	

1. He's not like his brother in any way. The two of them are _____completely_____ different.

2. Do you like to listen to the rain on the _____?

3. You can buy unusual _____ from other countries in that store.

4. Close your eyes and _____ that you're lying on a beautiful beach right now.

5. Can you really eat that _____ pizza? I don't believe it!

6. What's on TV tonight? Let's look in the newspaper and _____.

7. In the park, there are gardens with _____ walls all around them.

8. The ticket costs $8.00, but I have _____ $7.25.

9. When does the sun go down? What time does it _____ dark?

C **Read these sentences. Match the boldfaced target words with their definitions.**

a. She can **count** to ten in three languages.

b. Let's give them a book about **history**. They'll like that. They **collect** history books.

c. Los Angeles is in the western part of the United States. New York is in the **east**.

d. They have horses on their **farm**. Their **neighbors** have chickens and cows.

Target Words	Definitions
1. ___farm___	= a piece of land where people grow things and keep animals
2. _____	= find how many things are in a group (1, 2, 3 . . .)
3. _____	= people who live near you
4. _____	= get things of one kind and keep them together
5. _____	= where the sun comes up in the morning
6. _____	= the record of things that happened in the past

Building on the Vocabulary

Studying Collocations

Get can go together with many different words, and *get* has many meanings. After *get*, you will often see a noun *(Get a **job**!)* or an adjective *(Are you getting **tired**?)*. The words after *get* change its meaning.

A Read these sentences with *get*. In three sentences, *get* means *become*.
Check (✔) the sentences.

	GET = BECOME
1. Bob's getting some bread at the store.	
2. Your hair is getting long.	
3. He needs to get a job.	
4. Don't get angry!	
5. It gets dark early in the winter.	
6. Where can I get a bus to the airport?	

B Circle the words after *get* in the sentences in Part A. Which words are
adjectives? Which are nouns? Complete this statement:

In sentences with *get* + _____, the verb *get* means *become*.

C Write four sentences. Use *get* meaning *become*.

1. _____

2. _____

3. _____

4. _____

DEVELOPING YOUR SKILLS

Scanning

Read these questions about "San Marino." Scan the reading and write
short answers.

1. How big is San Marino? _____

2. What country is all around San Marino? _____

3. What are some farm products from San Marino? _____

4. What can you see in the center of the country? _____

5. How many people visit the country each year? _____

6. Why do people visit San Marino? Give two reasons.

a. _____ b. _____

Thinking about the Main Idea

What is the main idea of "San Marino"? Circle the answer.

1. San Marino is a tiny country, but it's interesting to many people.
2. Small countries sell their products to people from other countries.
3. You can walk across San Marino.

Discussion

Talk about these questions in a small group or with the whole class.

1. Visitors to San Marino sometimes buy stamps and coins as souvenirs. Souvenirs help people remember a visit to a place. Do you have any souvenirs from your travels?
2. What kind of souvenirs do you like?

Using New Words

Ask and answer these questions with a partner. Then talk about your answers with the class.

1. What country is to the **east** of us?
2. Do you **collect** anything? Would you like to **collect** something in the future?
3. Does your family have good **neighbors**? What do you like or dislike about them?
4. Would you like to live on a **farm**? Why or why not?
5. Can you name any **history** books or historical movies about?

Writing

Write a paragraph about your city or hometown. You can begin with:
I am from _____.

Tell where your city or hometown is. Answer these questions:

- How big is it or how many people live there?
- What is the weather like?
- Is it famous for one or more products?
- What do you like about your city or hometown?

CHAPTER 8

Mount Fuji

Evening Snow, Mt. Fuji by Toyokuni II

GETTING READY TO READ

Talk with your class.

1. How many people in the class know the name Fuji? Where is Mount Fuji?

2. Mount Fuji is a volcano. What kind of volcano do you think it is? Circle your answer.

   a. an **active** volcano (Sometimes it erupts. It sends out hot rock and lots of smoke.)

   b. a **dormant** volcano (It is quiet now, but it might erupt in the future.)

   c. an **extinct** volcano (It cannot erupt anymore.)

3. How many people in the class like to climb mountains?

READING

Look at the words and pictures next to the reading. Then read.

Mount Fuji

1   There is a very famous mountain in Japan. It's called Mount Fuji (or *Fuji-san*). People can see it from many parts of the country. It's more than 12,000 feet high, higher than any other mountain in Japan. It's wonderful to look at. Many people take photos of it. **Artists** often **draw** or **paint** pictures of it. They love the mountain's beautiful and unusual **shape**. It's symmetrical.[1]

2   Mount Fuji is **actually** a volcano. People often forget that fact. The last eruption[2] was a long time **ago**, in 1708. Now it's dormant (sleeping). People can safely **climb** to the top of it. More than 200,000 people climb Fuji each year. Most of them are Japanese. However, a large number—about 30% of them—come from **foreign** countries.

3   July and August are the **best** months to climb Mount Fuji. At other times during the year, it can be **dangerous**. There's too much snow and bad weather. Even in the summer, the climb isn't easy. The air is thin on the mountain, so it's hard to **breathe**. The sun is strong, and the days can be very hot. Then at night, it's cold.

4   Many climbers start up the mountain late in the day. They carry flashlights,[3] and they climb for hours in the dark. They want to arrive at the top before sunrise. Then they can watch the sun come up. It's getting to be[4] a Japanese **tradition**.

5   Many Japanese people want to climb Mount Fuji **once** in their lives. Most of them want to climb it only once. There is a saying[5] in Japan: "A person who never climbs Mount Fuji is a **fool**, and a person who climbs **twice** is twice the fool."

[1] *symmetrical* = with both halves exactly the same size and shape

[2] *eruption* = the action of a volcano sending out hot rock

[3] a *flashlight*

[4] *getting to be* = becoming

[5] *saying* = a famous statement that many people think is true

Quick Comprehension Check

Read these sentences. Circle T (true) or F (false).

1. Mount Fuji is in Japan.   T   F

2. Many people take photos of Mount Fuji.   T   F

3. No one can climb this mountain.   T   F

4. It never gets cold on Mount Fuji.   T   F

5. Some people go to the mountain top and watch the sun come up.   T   F

6. Many Japanese people like to drive up Mount Fuji.   T   F

EXPLORING VOCABULARY

Thinking about the Vocabulary

Which target words and phrases are new to you? Circle them here and in the reading. Then read "Mount Fuji" again. Look at the context of each new word and phrase. Can you guess the meaning?

Target Words and Phrases			
artists (1)	actually (2)	best (3)	once (5)
draw (1)	ago (2)	dangerous (3)	fool (5)
paint (1)	climb (2)	breathe (3)	twice (5)
shape (1)	foreign (2)	tradition (4)	

Using the Vocabulary

A Complete these sentences. Write *breathing hard, climbing a mountain, drawing a map,* or *doing something dangerous.*

1. He's _____.   2. He's _____.

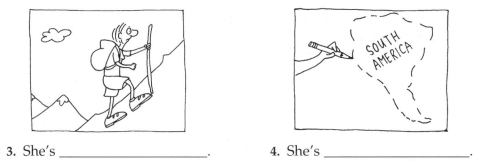

3. She's _____ .　　　4. She's _____ .

B These sentences are **about the reading**. Complete them with the words in the box.

actually	ago	artists	best	fools	foreign
once	painted	shape	traditions	twice	

1. Some people draw pictures of Mount Fuji. These people are

    _____ .

2. A Japanese artist _____ the picture on page 54.

3. Some people think Mount Fuji is all rock inside, but it's really not. Mount
    Fuji is _____ a volcano.

4. The last eruption of this volcano was a long time _____ (in
    the past). It was in 1708.

5. Most climbers on Mount Fuji are Japanese, but some climbers don't come
    from Japan. They come from _____ countries.

6. July and August are the _____ months to climb Mount Fuji.
    The other months are not as good.

7. Sometimes the people of a country do the same thing again and again,
    year after year. For example, they may do the same things every New
    Year's Day. These things are _____ .

8. Some people climb Mount Fuji only _____ (one time).

9. Others climb it _____ (two times).

10. Many Japanese think one trip up the mountain is enough. They say, "Only
    _____ climb it twice." They think those climbers are a little
    crazy.

C These sentences use the target words **in new contexts. Complete them with the words in the box.**

actually	ago	artist	best	fool	foreign
once	paint	shapes	tradition	twice	

1. Don't worry, I won't give them any more money. I won't make the same mistake again. I'm not a _____!

2. She collects stamps and coins from _____ countries.

3. Doug draws pictures for children's books. He's an excellent

   _____.

4. This kind of fruit doesn't look good to eat, but it _____ tastes great.

5. Some Chinese people wear red clothes for the New Year. It's a Chinese

   _____.

6. An orange doesn't look like a lemon. They have different colors and different _____.

7. Jessica says, "Toyota makes good cars. Saab makes better ones. Mercedes makes the _____ cars of all."

8. The baby arrived about eleven months _____. He's almost one year old.

9. We can take the test only _____. We get only one try.

10. Indira calls her parents _____ a week—on Wednesdays and Sundays.

11. I'm going to _____ my room blue and white.

Building on the Vocabulary

Studying Word Grammar

Nouns, verbs, and adjectives are examples of different kinds, or categories, of words. Each kind of word has a different use. All the different kinds of words are called the **parts of speech**.

A Label each category in the chart. Write *Adjectives*, *Verbs*, and *Nouns*.

_____	_____	_____
an artist	climb	best
ice	count	cool
a neighbor	draw	empty
a product	paint	safe
snow	protect	unusual

_____   _____   _____

_____   _____   _____

_____   _____   _____

_____   _____   _____

_____   _____   _____

B Add these words to the chart in Part A: *breathe, collect, dangerous, a fool, foreign, large, a shape, spell, a tradition.*

C Add two or more words of your own to each category in the chart in Part A.

DEVELOPING YOUR SKILLS

Understanding Sentences with *Because*

Sentences with *because* answer the question *why*.

A Choose the best way to complete each sentence. Write the letters.

_c_ 1. People can see Mount Fuji from many parts of Japan

____ 2. Artists like to draw and paint pictures of Mount Fuji

____ 3. This volcano is safe to climb

____ 4. July and August are the best months to climb Mount Fuji

____ 5. It's hard to breathe high on the mountain

____ 6. Many people climb at night

a. because it is dormant (sleeping).

b. because the air is thin.

c. because it's over 12,000 feet high.

d. because they want to be at the top at sunrise.

e. because it has a beautiful shape.

f. because the weather is good then.

B Complete this sentence.

I (would/wouldn't) like to climb Mount Fuji because . . .

Summarizing

Some of the information in this summary of the reading is wrong. Find and correct six mistakes. The first mistake is corrected for you.

> *mountain*
> Mount Fuji is a beautiful ~~island~~ in Japan. It's famous for its unusual history. More than 200,000 people drive to the top of it each year. July and August are the dangerous months to climb Mount Fuji. Most of the climbers are Japanese, but many come from Japan. Many climb the mountain at night so they can paint the sunrise.

Sharing Opinions

Think about the questions. Then talk with a partner.

1. What does this statement mean: "A person who never climbs Mount Fuji is a fool."?

   a. Only crazy people climb Mount Fuji.

   b. Everybody should climb Mount Fuji.

   Do you agree? Tell why or why not.

2. What does this statement mean: "A person who climbs Mount Fuji twice is twice the fool."?

   a. Only crazy people climb Mount Fuji twice.

   b. Everybody should climb Mount Fuji twice.

   Do you agree? Tell why or why not.

3. Some people say, "Everybody should climb Mount Fuji at some time in his or her life." Think of something else that is worth doing, and complete this statement: Everybody should _____ at some time in his or her life.

Using New Words

Work with a partner. Choose five target words or phrases from the list on page 56. On a piece of paper, use each word or phrase in a sentence.

Writing

Imagine a foreign visitor to your country wants your advice. He or she asks you: "Where should I go in your country? What should I see?" On a piece of paper, write six sentences. Begin each sentence with:
I think you should . . .

Wrap-up

REVIEWING VOCABULARY

A Match the words below with their definitions. There are three extra words.

along	below	count	dangerous	draw	else
~~however~~	land	product	shine	temperature	twice

1. _____however_____ = but

2. _____ = make a picture of (with pen or pencil)

3. _____ = under, at a lower point or place

4. _____ = a measure of how hot or cold something is

5. _____ = give or make light, like the sun

6. _____ = likely to hurt someone, not safe

7. _____ = tell how many there are of something (1, 2, 3, . . .)

8. _____ = something that people make or grow

9. _____ = by the side of

B Complete these sentences. Two words do not belong in the sentences.

belong to	completely	find out	foreign	government	imagine
large	of course	rock	such as	tradition	~~whole~~

1. He's inviting the _____whole_____ class to his house—all thirty people.

2. Americans usually have cake at birthday parties. It's a _____.

3. Lions, tigers, and house cats all _____ the cat family.

4. I don't know the answer. I will ask somebody and _____.

5. The bus is _____ full. No more people can get on it.

6. Many people from _____ countries visit San Marino.

7. _____ that you have one million dollars. Isn't that a nice idea?

8. Doctors tell us to eat fruit _____ apples, oranges, and bananas.

9. The president is the most important person in the _____.

10. Is it cold in Antarctica? Well, _____ it is!

EXPANDING VOCABULARY

A Each form of a word belongs to the same **word family**. Sometimes two words in a family look the same. Look at this chart.

NOUNS	VERBS	ADJECTIVES
climb	climb	
	cool	cool
	empty	empty
paint	paint	
touch	touch	

Now look at the **boldfaced** words in these sentences. Write *noun, verb,* or *adjective* after each word.

1. a. Do you sometimes **climb** mountains? _____verb_____

 b. It's a long **climb** to the top of Mount Fuji. _____

2. a. You can **cool** your drink with some ice. _____

 b. Would you like a **cool** drink? _____

3. a. My cup is **empty**. I have no more coffee. _____

 b. Please **empty** the dishwasher. _____

4. a. My neighbors are going to **paint** their house. _____

 b. They'll need a lot of **paint**. _____

5. a. Please don't **touch** the paintings. _____

 b. My finger is black and blue. It hurts to the **touch**. _____

B You know the words *ice, rock, scientist,* and *snow*. Look at the adjectives in their word families. Then, on a piece of paper, write four sentences with these four adjectives.

	NOUNS	VERBS	ADJECTIVES
1.	ice		icy
2.	a rock		rocky
3.	a scientist		scientific
4.	snow	snow	snowy

PLAYING WITH WORDS

There are ten target words from Unit 2 in this puzzle. The words go across (→) and down (↓). Find the words and circle them. Then use them to complete the sentences below.

1. Children study the _____history_____ of their country in school.

2. Their plane is here. It arrived ten minutes _____.

3. She's making a cake in the _____ of a heart.

4. Here are three pictures by that artist. Which is the _____ one?

5. He is a _____. He studies the oceans.

6. I go food shopping _____ a week, on Saturday.

7. It's not healthy to _____ smoke from cigarettes.

8. Their house is made of _____.

9. There's a hole in the _____ of the house, and rain is coming in.

10. There aren't many continents, _____ seven.

BUILDING DICTIONARY SKILLS

A Dictionaries use many **abbreviations**. An abbreviation is a short way to write a word. Can you write the abbreviations for these words? Check your answers in a dictionary.

1. Mister   M r .
2. Doctor   __ __.
3. Street   __ __.
4. New York   __ __
5. Saturday   __ __ __.
6. Post Office   __ __

B Dictionaries use abbreviations for **parts of speech**. Parts of speech are categories of words, such as *nouns, verbs,* and *adjectives.*

1. Look at the dictionary entries below. Find the abbreviations for *noun, verb,* and *adjective.* Circle them.

2. Look at your own dictionary. What abbreviations does it use for *noun, verb,* and *adjective?* Write them here: _____ _____ _____

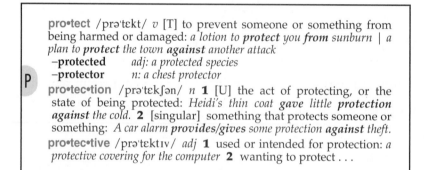

pro•tect /prəˈtɛkt/ *v* [T] to prevent someone or something from being harmed or damaged: *a lotion to* **protect** *you* **from** *sunburn* | *a plan to* **protect** *the town* **against** *another attack*
–**protected**   *adj: a protected species*
–**protector**   *n: a chest protector*
pro•tec•tion /prəˈtɛkʃən/ *n* **1** [U] the act of protecting, or the state of being protected: *Heidi's thin coat* **gave** *little* **protection** **against** *the cold.* **2** [singular] something that protects someone or something: *A car alarm* **provides/gives** *some protection* **against** *theft.*
pro•tec•tive /prəˈtɛktɪv/ *adj* **1** used or intended for protection: *a protective covering for the computer* **2** wanting to protect . . .

C These words are related to target words from Unit 2. What parts of speech are they? Write abbreviations for their parts of speech.

1. actual _____ adj. _____

ac•tu•al /ˈæktʃuəl, ˈækʃuəl/ *adj* real, especially when compared with what is believed, expected, or intended: *Were those his actual words? . . .*

2. collector _____

col•lec•tor /kəˈlɛktɚ/ *n* **1** someone whose job is to collect things: *a tax collector* **2** someone who collects things for pleasure: *a rock collector*

3. foolish _____

fool•ish /ˈfulɪʃ/ *adj* **1** not sensible or wise: *It would be* **foolish of** *them* **to** *start fighting over this.* **2** silly or . . .

4. shiny _____

shin•y /ˈʃaɪni/ *adj* bright and smooth looking: *shiny hair* | *shiny leather boots*

UNIT 3

OUR BODIES

Mmm, this tastes good!

CHAPTER 9

Your Sense of Taste

GETTING READY TO READ

Talk with a partner.

1. **a.** What tastes good to you? Write a list of things you like to eat. (Write fast! You have one minute.)

   b. Show your list to your partner. On your lists, circle the things you both like.

2. **a.** Do you have a sweet tooth? (This means: Do you like candy, chocolate, desserts, and other sweet things?)

   b. Find out how many people in the class have a sweet tooth.

READING

Look at the words and pictures next to the reading. Then read without stopping. Don't worry about new words. Don't stop to use a dictionary. Just keep reading!

Your Sense of Taste

1   **Taste** is one of our five **senses**. The others are hearing, **sight**, touch, and **smell**. You hear with your ears, you see with your eyes, and you taste things with your tongue.[1]

[1] a *tongue*

2   On your tongue, you have groups of tiny taste buds. Taste buds send information about food to your **brain**. You have a lot of taste buds, maybe even 10,000! People don't all have the same number of them. Women often have more taste buds than men.

[2] Lemons are *sour.*

3   Because of your taste buds, foods like ice cream and bananas taste **sweet**. French fries, cheese, and ocean water taste **salty**. Lemons have a sour[2] taste, and coffee is bitter.[3] Most people know about these four main tastes: sweet, salty, sour, and bitter. But scientists now know about a fifth **one**, umami. We can taste this one in some kinds of cheese, meat, and mushrooms.[4] *Umami* is a Japanese word. It means something like good-tasting.

[3] Coffee with no sugar is *bitter.*

4   People can lose their sense of taste. For example, a person with a cold sometimes can't breathe through his or her **nose**. Different foods may all taste the same. Why does this happen? There is a close **relationship** between our sense of taste and our sense of smell. Each sense **affects** the other.

[4] *mushrooms*

5   The feel and temperature of food also affect its taste. Tastes aren't as strong in very hot or very cold foods. For example, very cold, hard ice cream is not as sweet as not-so-cold, soft ice cream. Also, sometimes a food tastes good only at the right temperature. **Consider** your favorite cold drink. Does it taste good hot, **too**? Lots of people love cold Coca-Cola but **can't stand** it hot!

6   Why does a sense of taste **matter**? For one thing, it helps people decide on safe things to eat. And of course, thanks to[5] your sense of taste, you can enjoy all your favorite foods.

[5] *thanks to =* because of

Quick Comprehension Check

Read these sentences. Circle T (true) or F (false).

1. People have five senses: taste, hearing, sight, smell, and touch. T F

2. You might have 10,000 taste buds on your tongue. T F

3. Taste buds send information to your stomach. T F

4. There are only four main tastes: sweet, salty, sour, and bitter. T F

5. The feel and temperature of food affect its taste. T F

6. Nobody actually needs a sense of taste. T F

EXPLORING VOCABULARY

Thinking about the Vocabulary

Which target words and phrases are new to you? Circle them here and in the reading. Then read "Your Sense of Taste" again. Look at the context of each new word and phrase. Can you guess the meaning?

Target Words and Phrases			
taste (1)	brain (2)	nose (4)	too (5)
senses (1)	sweet (3)	relationship (4)	can't stand (5)
sight (1)	salty (3)	affects (4)	matter (6)
smell (1)	one (3)	consider (5)	

Using the Vocabulary

Ⓐ **Complete these sentences. Use the nouns *brain, ears, eyes, nose, senses, sight, smell,* and *taste*. Use the verbs *taste* and *smell*.**

1. Tom has five ____senses____: hearing, touch, _____, _____, and _____.

2. This is Tom's _____.

3. He uses his _____ to hear things.

4. Tom uses his _____ to see things.

5. He uses his _____ to _____ things.

6. He uses his tongue to _____ things.

B These sentences are **about the reading**. Complete them with the words and phrases in the box.

affect	can't stand	consider	matters	ones	relationship	salty	sweet	too

1. People have five senses. One is taste. The other _____ are sight, hearing, smell, and touch.
2. Desserts such as ice cream, cake, and candy are _____ things. There is sugar in them.
3. French fries, cheese, and ocean water all have a _____ taste.
4. The temperature of a food can _____, or change, the way it tastes.
5. Your sense of smell affects your sense of taste. There's a close _____ between these two senses.
6. Some foods taste good hot, and they taste good cold, _____. Other foods are good only at one temperature.
7. For example, _____ cold drinks. Think of your favorite one.
8. Many people love cold Coca-Cola. But do they like hot Coke? No, they _____ it!
9. A sense of taste is important. It _____.

C These sentences use the target words and phrases **in new contexts**. Complete them with the words in the box.

affects	can't stand	consider	matter	ones	relationship	salty	sweet	too

1. Bob and Mary are happily married. They have a good _____.
2. I never read history books. I _____ them. They put me to sleep.
3. A cold usually _____ your breathing and your senses of taste and smell.
4. I need something to drink. This pizza is very _____.
5. I put sugar or honey in my tea. I like _____ tea.
6. Paul collects stamps. He has many kinds of stamps, but his favorites are the foreign _____.

7. We can go down Main Street or Park Avenue. It doesn't _____.
It's the same distance.

8. I like sweet foods, and I like salty ones, _____.

9. His job is dangerous. He should _____ getting a new one.

Building on the Vocabulary

Studying Word Grammar

The word *one* can be a **pronoun**. Remember: Pronouns (such as *I, he, him, it, they, them*) take the place of nouns. We can use *one* and *ones* for people or things:

Notes	Examples
• *One* can take the place of *a/an* + singular noun.	She has a car, but I don't have ~~a car.~~ *one*
• *Ones* can take the place of a plural noun.	These books are John's. The ~~books~~ *ones* on the table are mine.
• *One* or *ones* can be used with an adjective.	You have small ears. I have big **ones**!
• *One* is often used with *this* or *that*.	I don't like that car, but this **one** is nice.

Look for a noun that is used twice. Change the second noun to *one* or *ones*.

1. He's reading a book. It's a very long ~~book~~. *one*

2. Ms. Summers is an artist, and she's a very good artist.

3. Hannah has an older brother and two younger brothers.

4. Make a list of products from your country. Which are the most important products?

5. That bag belongs to Steve, and this bag is Barbara's.

6. There are a lot of small islands in the Galápagos and thirteen larger islands.

7. Asia is the largest continent. The smallest continents are Australia and Europe.

DEVELOPING YOUR SKILLS

Scanning

A **Where is the information about these topics in "Your Sense of Taste"? Scan the reading on page 67. Write the paragraph number (1–6).**

_3_ **a.** the five main tastes

_____ **b.** the five senses

_____ **c.** why a sense of taste is important

_____ **d.** temperature and taste

_____ **e.** what taste buds do

_____ **f.** taste and smell

B **Write a sentence about each of the six topics from paragraphs 1–6. Use information from the reading.**

1.   _The five senses are taste, touch, hearing, sight, and smell._

2.   _____

3.   _____

4.   _____

5.   _____

6.   _____

Summarizing

Some of the information in this summary of the reading is wrong. Find and correct five mistakes. The first one is corrected for you.

                    senses
Taste is one of our five ~~feelings.~~ The other ones are hearing, touch, smell,

and eyes. You smell things with the thousands of taste buds on your tongue.

Taste buds send information to your nose. Several things can touch the taste of

foods, such as the feel or temperature of the food or having a cold.

Sharing Opinions

A Which of the five senses is most important to you? Write number 1 next to it in the chart. Which one is the least important? Write number 5 next to it. Number the other ones in order of importance.

B Talk with others in a small group. Find out their opinions. Complete the chart.

THE 5 SENSES	YOU	_____ (name)	_____ (name)	_____ (name)
Sense of hearing				
Sense of sight				
Sense of smell				
Sense of taste				
Sense of touch				

Using New Words

Work with a partner. Choose five target words and phrases from the list on page 68. Write five sentences.

Writing

Sometimes the taste or smell of something makes us remember a place or a person. Write a paragraph about a taste or smell like that. You can begin with: *The (smell/taste) of* _____ *makes me think of . . .* Write four or more sentences.

CHAPTER 10

Bones

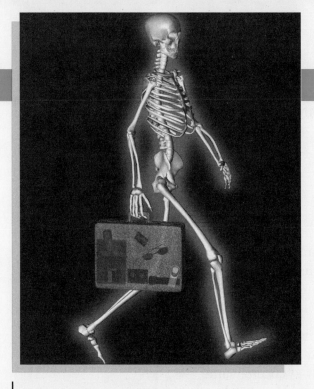

The bones in the human body

GETTING READY TO READ

Talk with a partner or in a small group.

1. Make a list of names for body parts (*head, legs, eyes, . . .*). Write fast! You have two minutes.

2. Look at your list. Which body parts have bones in them? Circle them.

3. How many bones are there in your body?
   a. 102   **b.** 145   **c.** 206

4. How many joints[1] are there in your body?
   a. 52   **b.** more than 70   **c.** over 100

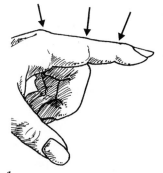

[1] Bones come together at *joints.*

READING

Look at the words and pictures next to the reading. Then read.

Bones

1   Imagine your body with no **bones**. It's not a pretty picture,[1] is it?

2   We need our bones. They **support** our bodies so we can stand. They also protect soft parts inside us. For example, the bones in your head form the skull. The skull protects your brain. Your ribs protect your heart.

3   The bones in your body **make up** your skeleton.[2] Your skeleton has long bones (in your arms and legs) and short bones (such as the ones in your fingers). It even has some tiny bones. (They're in the part of the ear inside your head.) So, how many do you have in all? There are 206 bones.

4   In many places, two bones come together. There are **joints** at these places. Your **knees** are the joints **in the middle** of your legs. Your **elbows** are the joints in the middle of your arms. You need joints to move and **bend**. The **human** body has more than 70 joints.

5   Your elbow and your **shoulder** are examples of two different **types** of joints. Your arm can bend at the elbow, but it can bend just one way. At the shoulder, your arm can move freely up, down, left, right—all around. There are other types of joints, too. For example, babies have joints between the eight bones that make up the skull (the bones of the head). These bones then grow together, so in older children and **adults**, the joints don't move.

6   Sometimes people have problems with their joints, especially older adults. Doctors have ways to **fix** many of these problems. They can even put in a new knee or hip.[3] These artificial[4] joints are usually **metal** or **plastic**. Doctors can also fix bones that break. But it's best to keep your skeleton in good health! Are you **taking care of** yours?

[1] *not a pretty picture* = not nice to look at or think about

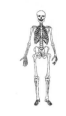

[2] a human *skeleton*

[3] a *hip* = the joint where the leg connects to the rest of the body

[4] *artificial* = not natural, made by people

Quick Comprehension Check

Read these sentences. Circle T (true) or F (false).

1. There are about 100 bones in the human body.   T   F

2. Bones hold up our bodies so we can stand.   T   F

3. Bones come together at joints.   T   F

4. We have joints to protect the soft parts inside our bodies.   T   F

5. There are different kinds of joints.   T   F

6. Doctors use old bones to make new joints.   T   F

EXPLORING VOCABULARY

Thinking about the Vocabulary

Which target words and phrases are new to you? Circle them here and in the reading. Then read "Bones" again. Look at the context of each new word and phrase. Can you guess the meaning?

Target Words and Phrases			
bones (1)	**knees** (4)	**human** (4)	**fix** (6)
support (2)	**in the middle** (4)	**shoulder** (5)	**metal** (6)
make up (3)	**elbows** (4)	**types** (5)	**plastic** (6)
joints (4)	**bend** (4)	**adults** (5)	**taking care of** (6)

Using the Vocabulary

A **Complete the sentence. Then label the picture. Write** *bones, elbow, joints, knee,* **and** *shoulder.*

1. The _____human_____ body has 206 _____.

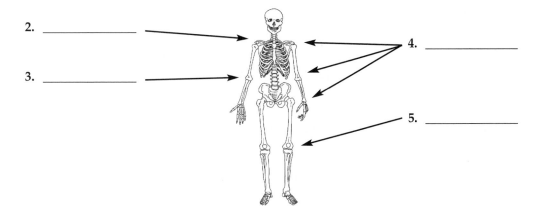

2. _____

3. _____

4. _____

5. _____

B These sentences are **about the reading**. Complete them with the words and phrases in the box.

adults	bend	fix	in the middle	make up
metal	plastic	support	taking care of	types

1. The bones in a person's body _____ his or her skeleton. (Together, they form the skeleton.)

2. We need our bones. They _____ our bodies. They hold us up.

3. Your elbows are the joints _____ of your arms. They are at the center, or the halfway point, in your arms.

4. Because you have joints, you can _____ your legs. (You don't have to keep them straight.) Then you can run, jump, and dance.

5. There are several kinds of joints. Your elbows and shoulders are examples of two different _____.

6. Babies have joints between the bones in their heads. The heads of babies are different from the heads of _____.

7. People sometimes break bones, or they have problems with their joints. But doctors can often _____ them.

8. Doctors can even put in a new joint made of _____ (a hard, usually shiny material).

9. Some new joints are _____ (a strong, light material made using chemicals).

10. Are you _____ your bones? What can you do to protect them?

C These sentences use the target words and phrases **in new contexts**. Complete them with the words and phrases in the box.

adult	bend	fixes	in the middle	makes up
metal	plastic	support	takes care of	type

1. Keep your legs straight—don't _____ your knees—and try to touch the floor.

2. Sometimes I have bad dreams and I wake up _____ of the night.

3. When does a young person become an _____?

4. The walls of a house _____ the roof.

5. What _____ of exercise do you like best?

6. Sometimes Don and Eva are both at work. Then a baby-sitter

   _____ their baby.

7. Ed is an automobile mechanic. He works at a garage and he

   _____ cars.

8. Some car parts are plastic, but car engines are made of _____.

9. People buy soda in clear _____ bottles and shiny metal cans.

10. Water _____ two-thirds (2/3) of the human body.

Building on the Vocabulary

Studying Collocations

Make up is a **phrasal verb**. Phrasal verbs have two parts: a verb (such as *make, get, turn*) and a particle (such as *up, out, off*). In Units 1 and 2, you learned the phrasal verbs *find out, go on,* and *look up.*

A **Complete these sentences with the phrasal verbs *make up, find out, go on, or look up.***

1. You can _____ that word in the dictionary.

2. Foreign students _____ 15% of the Class of 2006.

3. I hope the neighbors' party doesn't _____ all night!

4. What's happening across the street? Let's go and _____.

B **Write your own sentences with the four phrasal verbs in Part A.**

1. _____

2. _____

3. _____

4. _____

DEVELOPING YOUR SKILLS

Scanning

Read these questions about "Bones." Scan the reading and write short answers.

1. Why do we need our bones? Give two reasons. _____

   _____

   _____

2. How many bones are in the human skeleton? _____

3. How many joints are there? _____

4. Why do we need joints? _____

5. Where in the body can you find tiny bones? _____

6. What are two examples of different kinds of joints? _____

   _____

7. What is one difference between babies and adults? _____

   _____

8. What are artificial joints made of? _____

Thinking about the Main Idea

What is the main idea of "Bones"? Circle the answer.

1. We need our bones and joints so we can stand and move.
2. There are over seventy joints in the human body.
3. Older people should take care of their bones.

Discussion

A **Read the questions in the chart on page 79. Write *yes, no,* or a question mark *(?)* if you don't know.**

	YOU	_____ (name)	_____ (name)
1. Do you eat enough foods with calcium (from milk, cheese, yogurt, ice cream) for strong bones?			
2. Do you get enough vitamin D (from milk or sunlight)?			
3. Do you get enough exercise?			
4. Do you usually eat well?			
5. Is it hard for you to eat the right foods?			

B Talk with two other people about the questions on the chart. Find out their answers. Complete the chart and talk about your answers with the class.

Using New Words

Ask and answer these questions with a partner. Use one of the words in parentheses. Then talk about your answers with the class.

1. Can you name five **types** of (fruit/animals)?
2. Can you name three things made of (**metal/plastic**)?
3. Do you ever fall asleep **in the middle** of a (movie/class)?
4. When does a (girl/boy) become an **adult**?

Writing

You know it's important to have a good diet (to eat well) for strong bones and a healthy body. Do you think it's hard to eat well? Are you happy with your diet? Is there anything you would like to change? Write a paragraph of five or more sentences about eating well. You can begin with: *My diet these days is (good/okay/bad).*

CHAPTER 11

Blood

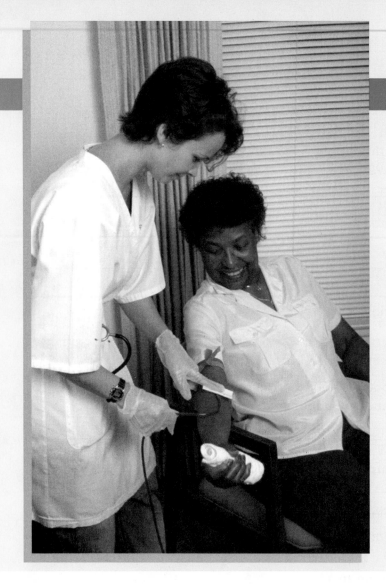

Giving blood

GETTING READY TO READ

Talk with your whole class.

1. What do you see in the photo?
2. Do you know any people who give blood?
3. There are four main types of blood. How many people in the class know their blood type?

    _____ out of _____ (total) people

READING

Look at the words next to the reading. Then read.

Blood

1   Some people can't stand the sight of **blood**. They hate to see their own blood, and they don't want to look at anyone else's blood, **either**!

2   Liz Kim **doesn't mind** the sight of blood. She **is used to** it. Liz is a **nurse**, and she sees blood every day. She works in a U.S. hospital. It's her job to take blood from blood donors.[1]

3   Hospitals keep blood in blood banks. Liz says, "Hospitals need to have blood ready for **emergencies**. People may need blood for a lot of **reasons**. For example, someone might come to the hospital after a car **accident** and need blood. Also, a doctor might have to give blood to a **patient** during surgery.[2] In this country, about four million people need a blood transfusion[3] each year." The new blood has to be a good **match** for the patient's own blood type.

4   The four main blood types are A, B, AB, and O.

- People with type A can give blood to people with type A or AB.
- People with type B can give blood to people with B or AB.
- People with type AB can give blood only to other people with AB. However, they can **receive** A, B, AB, or O type blood. They're **lucky**!
- Type O blood is **special**: People with type O can give blood to anyone. But they can receive blood only from other people with type O.

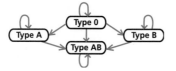

5   Not many people give blood. In the United States, only one out of twenty adults gives blood. Some people can't give blood for health reasons. Some are **too** nervous. Many people just never consider it. "Giving blood helps others," says Liz Kim. "It's also **good for** your heart. Please, think about it!"

[1] *blood donor* = a person who gives (or donates) blood

[2] *surgery* = the act of cutting open someone's body to fix something

[3] *blood transfusion* = the act of putting new blood into someone's body

Quick Comprehension Check

Read these sentences. Circle T (true) or F (false).

1. Liz Kim doesn't like to look at blood.   T   F

2. There are four main types of blood.   T   F

3. A person's blood type doesn't matter at all.   T   F

4. Everyone can give blood to everyone else.   T   F

5. Only a few adults in the United States give blood.   T   F

6. Liz Kim wants people to give blood.   T   F

EXPLORING VOCABULARY

Thinking about the Vocabulary

Which target words and phrases are new to you? Circle them here and in the reading. Then read "Blood" again. Look at the context of each new word and phrase. Can you guess the meaning?

Target Words and Phrases

blood (1)	emergencies (3)	receive (4)
either (1)	reasons (3)	lucky (4)
doesn't mind (2)	accident (3)	special (4)
is used to (2)	patient (3)	too (5)
nurse (2)	match (3)	good for (5)

Using the Vocabulary

Ⓐ **These sentences are about the reading. Complete them with the words and phrases in the box.**

don't mind	either	emergency	good for	is used to
lucky	match	receive	special	too

1. Some people can't stand the sight of their own blood. They don't want to see anyone else's blood, _____.

2. For other people, the sight of blood isn't so bad. It doesn't really matter to them. They _____ it.

3. Liz sees blood all the time. Liz _____ it, so she doesn't mind it.

4. Sometimes a person is hurt and loses a lot of blood. In an
   _____ like this, the person needs new blood fast.

5. Any new blood has to be like a person's own blood. It must be a good
   _____ for their own blood.

6. Hospitals _____ blood from blood donors.

7. People with type AB blood can receive type A, B, AB, or O. When they
   need blood, it's easy to find. So they're _____.

8. People with type O blood can give it to anyone. In this way, type O is
   different from all the other types. It's _____.

9. Some people are nervous about giving blood, but they can do it. Other
   people are _____ nervous, so they can't do it.

10. Giving blood helps a person's heart. It's _____ the heart.

B These sentences use the target words and phrases **in new contexts.**
Complete them with the words in the box.

are used to	don't mind	either	emergency	good for
lucky	match	receives	special	too

1. Sure, you can look at my book. I _____.

2. Alan's orange tie is not a good _____ for his green shirt.

3. Nancy _____ birthday presents from her friends.

4. Susan has a bad cut on her hand. We have take her to the
   _____ room at the hospital.

5. I don't want to do just the usual tonight. Let's do something
   _____.

6. The fish soup doesn't look good, and it doesn't smell good,
   _____!

7. My parents are nervous about flying, but my brothers and I
   _____ it. We often travel by plane.

8. Eat your vegetables! They're _____ you.

9. Al was in an accident, but he wasn't hurt. He was _____.

10. That movie is for adults only. Jack can't go to it. He's 13, so he's
    _____ young.

C **Read these sentences. Match the boldfaced target words with their definitions.**

a. Students can get health information from the school **nurse**.

b. Even careful drivers sometimes have **accidents**.

c. The doctor's waiting room is full of **patients**.

d. He sometimes leaves work early without giving any **reason**.

e. She cut her hand on some glass, and there was a lot of **blood**.

Target Words   **Definitions**

1. ___reason___ = the cause of something (why it happens)

2. _____ = the red liquid that moves through your body

3. _____ = a person who takes care of sick or hurt people

4. _____ = people who get care from a doctor or nurse

5. _____ = bad things that happen by chance (they are not planned)

Building on the Vocabulary

Studying Word Grammar

In Chapter 1, you learned that *too* can mean *also*. For example:
  My elbow hurts, and my shoulder hurts, **too**.
  Doctors help patients, and nurses do, **too**.

Do not use *too* meaning *also* in negative sentences. Use *either*. For example:
  Jack's **not** here, and Sam is**n't, either**.
  My knees do**n't** hurt, and my feet do**n't, either**.

Complete these sentences. Use *too* or *either*.

1. A cold can affect your breathing and your sense of smell, _____.

2. He's not a fool, and she isn't, _____.

3. I can't buy a new car or a used one, _____.

4. I like the shape of that car and the color, _____.

5. I can't climb that mountain, and you can't, _____.

6. He's taking history courses, and he's studying foreign languages, _____.

7. His brother can fix cars and motorcycles, _____.

8. That girl doesn't eat well, and her friends don't, _____.

DEVELOPING YOUR SKILLS

Understanding Sentences with *Because*

 A Choose the best way to complete each sentence. Write the letters.

__d__ 1. Liz Kim doesn't mind the sight of blood

_____ 2. She sees blood every day

_____ 3. Hospitals must have blood ready

_____ 4. You can't receive just anyone's blood

_____ 5. Type O blood is special

_____ 6. People with type AB are lucky

a. because new blood must match your own.

b. because people with any blood type can use it.

c. because she works with blood donors.

d. because she's used to it.

e. because they can receive type A, B, AB, or O.

f. because patients may need it.

B Complete this sentence.

People give blood because _____

_____.

Summarizing

A These seven sentences make up a summary of the reading. Number the sentences in order.

_____ a. The blood they give stays in the hospital blood bank.

_____ b. For example, people with type O blood can receive only type O.

__1__ c. Liz Kim is a hospital nurse.

_____ d. The blood that patients receive must be a match for their own blood.

_____ e. She takes blood from donors.

__7__ f. Liz wants more people to give blood.

_____ g. The blood bank keeps it for patients who need a transfusion.

B Write the sentences in Part A as a paragraph.

_____

_____

_____

_____

_____

_____

_____

Sharing Opinions

Do you think you should give blood? Discuss your ideas and feelings in a small group. Then talk about them with the class.

Using New Words

Work with a partner. Take turns asking for and giving information. Then tell the class something about your partner.

1. Tell me something that's **good for** your health.
2. Tell me a kind of present you like to **receive**.
3. Tell me something that's hard for you to get **used to**.
4. Tell me about a **special** person in your life.

Writing

Does a nurse have a good job or a bad job? Write a paragraph about nurses. You can begin with: _Nurses have_ _____ _jobs._ Give the reasons for your opinion.

CHAPTER 12

Can You Give Me a Hand?

GETTING READY TO READ

Sometimes a group of words has a special meaning. This meaning is not the same as the usual meanings of the words. A group of words like this is an *idiom*.

A **Which four sentences below do you think have idioms? Check (✔) them.**

   ✔   **1.** He wants a shoulder to cry on.

_____ **2.** He'll give you a hand.

_____ **3.** He needs to wash his hands.

_____ **4.** The teacher has eyes in the back of his head.

_____ **5.** The teacher is keeping an eye on the students.

B **Match the idioms in Part A with their meanings. Write the numbers.**

   4   **a.** He sees everything that happens in class.

_____ **b.** He wants someone to listen to his problems.

_____ **c.** He will help you.

_____ **d.** He's watching the students.

READING

Look at the words and picture next to the reading. Then read.

Can You Give Me a Hand?

1.   An **idiom** is a group of words with a special meaning. The words in the idiom do not have their usual, **ordinary** meanings. Together, the words mean something different. English is full of idioms. You know some already, and you will **certainly** learn more.

2.   Many idioms **mention** parts of the body: the head, the hands, the heart, **and so on**. You might hear someone say, "My brother's getting a big head." The boy's head isn't growing! *A big head* is an idiom. This boy thinks he's very important and special. His sister doesn't think he is. She says that he's getting too **confident**.

3.   A friend might tell you, "Be careful. That girl has a big mouth."[1] The literal[2] meaning is *That girl's mouth is large.* However, *have a big mouth* is also an idiom. Your friend means the girl talks too much or she tells other people's **secrets**. Your friend is giving you some **advice**: You shouldn't tell that girl any **private** information. You can't **trust** her to keep quiet.[3]

4.   Take a guess at the meanings of these three sentences. Each sentence has an idiom. Each idiom mentions the heart but has nothing to do with[4] the heart.

   1. She knows the words to that song by heart.

   2. My heart was in my mouth.

   3. He has a heart of **gold**.

Did you **figure out** the meanings of the sentences? Here they are:

   1. She can remember the words to that song very well.

   2. I was very afraid.

   3. He is very good and **kind** to other people.

[1] a *mouth*

[2] *literal* = following the usual meaning of the words

[3] *keep quiet* = not say anything

[4] *has nothing to do with* = has no relationship to

5   There are idioms in every language. A few idioms in your first language may be the same in English. For example, for some Spanish speakers, *a heart of gold* is the same in Spanish, *un corazón de oro*.

6   The meaning of an idiom isn't always **clear**. So **perhaps** you'll want to buy a dictionary of idioms. That might be a good idea. Just don't pay an arm and a leg for it.

Quick Comprehension Check

Read these sentences. Circle T (true) or F (false).

1. An idiom is a group of words with a special meaning.	T	F
2. There are just a few idioms in English.	T	F
3. The idiom *have a big mouth* means *talk too much*.	T	F
4. A person with a heart of gold is very nervous.	T	F
5. Sometimes an idiom is the same in two different languages.	T	F
6. There are no dictionaries of English idioms.	T	F

EXPLORING VOCABULARY

Thinking about the Vocabulary

Which target words and phrases are new to you? Circle them here and in the reading. Then read "Can You Give Me a Hand?" again. Look at the context of each new word and phrase. Can you guess the meaning?

Target Words and Phrases			
idiom (1)	**and so on** (2)	**private** (3)	**kind** (4)
ordinary (1)	**confident** (2)	**trust** (3)	**clear** (6)
certainly (1)	**secrets** (3)	**gold** (4)	**perhaps** (6)
mention (2)	**advice** (3)	**figure out** (4)	

Using the Vocabulary

A These sentences are **about the reading**. Complete them with the words and phrases in the box.

certainly	clear	figure out	gold	idiom	mention	secrets	trust

1. Sometimes a group of words has a special meaning. For example, *have a sweet tooth* isn't about teeth. It means *like to eat sweet things.* It's an

   _____.

2. You can be sure that you will learn many idioms. You will

   _____ hear them in conversation.

3. Many English idioms _____ parts of the body such as the eyes or hands or heart.

4. Sometimes we don't tell other people about an idea or a plan, or we quietly tell just a few people. Ideas or plans like these are _____.

5. You can't _____ someone with a big mouth to keep a secret. You can't feel sure of this person.

6. You could say someone *has a heart of* _____. This special kind of metal is worth a lot of money.

7. Take time to think about something, and maybe then you can understand it. Sometimes, however, you just can't _____ the meaning of an idiom.

8. The meanings of some idioms are easy to understand. When the meaning isn't _____, try your dictionary.

B These sentences use the target words and phrases **in new contexts**. Complete them with the words and phrases in the box.

certainly	clear	figure out	gold	idiom	mention	secret	trust

1. Some kinds of metal are expensive, such as silver and _____.

2. My math homework is very difficult. I'll need help to _____ the problems.

3. Don't believe his story. You can't _____ him.

4. Don't tell anyone about their relationship. They want to keep it a

   _____.

5. There's a story about the accident in the newspaper, but it doesn't

   _____ the boy's name.

6. Of course we'll invite Rubaba. We _____ want her to come.

7. This book tells how to make bread. There are pictures, too. So the way to

   make bread is very _____.

8. My guess is that *put your foot in your mouth* is an _____.

C Read these sentences. Match the **boldfaced** target words with their definitions.

a. Today is no **ordinary** day. It's my twenty-first birthday!

b. A **private** room at the hospital costs a lot.

c. He won't listen to me, but **perhaps** he'll take your **advice**.

d. Thanks for your help. It was very **kind** of you.

e. They sell dairy products: milk, cheese, butter, **and so on**.

f. You don't seem nervous about the test. You seem **confident**.

Target Words   **Definitions**

1. _____ = maybe

2. _____ = and more things of the same kind

3. _____ = an opinion or idea about what someone should do

4. _____ = sure that you can do something

5. _____ = nice, friendly, and helpful

6. _____ = usual, not special in any way

7. _____ = not open for use by other people

Building on the Vocabulary

Studying Word Grammar

There are **count nouns** and **noncount nouns** in English.

Notes	**Examples**
• Count nouns have a singular form and a plural form.	I have one **book**. He has two **books**. I see a **man**. I see several **men**.
• Noncount nouns have only one form.	The **air** is hot.
Don't use *a, an,* or a number before a noncount noun. Don't add *–(e)s*.	Do we have a **homework**? They get a lot of snows.

A Complete the chart. Write each noncount noun in the right category:

advice	education	history	love	science
blood	exercise	ice	milk	tea
cheese	fun	information	music	time
coffee	gold	land	plastic	water

Liquids	_blood_	_____	_____	_____	_____
Solids	_cheese_	_____	_____	_____	_____
Ideas, things you can't touch	_advice_	_____	_____	_____	_____
	_____	_____	_____	_____	_____

B Write four sentences with a noncount noun + singular verb.

1. ___Milk is good for your bones._____

2. _____

3. _____

4. _____

DEVELOPING YOUR SKILLS

Scanning

Read these questions about "Can You Give Me a Hand?" Scan the reading. Write short answers.

1. What's an idiom? _____

2. What do many English idioms mention? _____

3. What does the idiom *have a big mouth* mean? _____

4. Complete these idioms:
   a. know something _____
   b. have your heart in your _____
   c. have a heart _____

5. What can you buy to help you understand idioms? _____

Thinking about the Main Idea

What is the main idea of "Can You Give Me a Hand?" Circle the answer.

1. The English language is full of idioms, and many of them mention parts of the body.
2. English is not the only language with idioms.
3. There are three idioms about the heart, but they really mean something else.

Discussion

Talk about these questions in a small group or with the whole class.

1. Is *getting a big head* a good thing or a bad thing? Tell why.
2. The reading says *don't pay an arm and a leg* for an idioms dictionary. Tell what you think this means.
3. What do you think *have a heart of stone* means?
4. Does your dictionary give you any help with idioms? Look up the word *heart* in your dictionary. Does it mention any idioms with *heart*?

Using New Words

Work with a partner. Choose five target words or phrases from the list on page 89. On a piece of paper, use each word or phrase in a sentence.

Writing

Write a paragraph about a person you know. You can begin with: *I think ___(name)___ has (a heart of gold/a big head/a big mouth/eyes in the back of his/her head).* Then give your reasons for saying this about the person.

Wrap-up

REVIEWING VOCABULARY

A Write these words in the chart below: *adult, elbow, knee, nose, nurse, patient, shoulder, sight, smell, taste.*

1.	Body parts	
2.	People	
3.	Senses	

B Complete these sentences with the phrases in the box.

can't stand	doesn't matter	doesn't mind	figure out	good for
in the middle	make up	take care of	used to	

1. Many different parts _____ an airplane: the engine(s), the wings, the tail, and so on.

2. My new job starts at 7:00 A.M. I'll have to get _____ getting up early.

3. Children should drink milk. It's _____ them.

4. I _____ green vegetables. No green beans, broccoli, or spinach for me!

5. My father sometimes falls asleep _____ of a movie.

6. Hannah is going to the beach for the weekend. Who will _____ her cat?

7. There was a bad car accident. The police are trying to _____ why it happened.

8. We can use Dan's car. It's OK with him. He _____.

9. Do you want to go to the 7:00 movie or the 9:00 one? It _____ to me.

EXPANDING VOCABULARY

A A **prefix** added to the beginning of a word changes its meaning. For example, the prefix *un-* means *not.* So *unhappy* means *not happy.*

Add the prefix *un-* to each of the adjectives in the box. Complete the sentences with the new words.

clear	healthy	important	kind	lucky	safe	usual

1. Don't worry about the distance. It doesn't matter. It's completely
   ___unimportant___ .

2. There are some _____ types of animals in the Galápagos.
   They're very special.

3. She looks _____. Is she eating well? Is she getting enough sleep?

4. That wasn't a nice thing to say to her. Don't be so _____!

5. The number *13* makes some people nervous. They think it's _____.

6. Don't take that road through the mountains. It's _____. You
   might have an accident.

7. I don't understand his plan. It's _____ what he's going to do.

B **Remember: Some words often go together, and some words *cannot* go together. One phrase in each group doesn't belong. It doesn't go with the verb. Cross it out.**

1. take (a guess/~~a relationship~~/someone's advice)

2. break (your nose/a bone/blood)

3. tell (a secret/the middle/the reason for something)

4. bend your (knees/brain/finger)

5. give (blood/an accident/some advice)

6. receive (a call from someone/a letter/an emergency)

C **Write six sentences using verb + noun combinations from Part B.**

1. ___How old is she? Take a guess.___
2. _____
3. _____
4. _____
5. _____
6. _____

PLAYING WITH WORDS

Complete the sentences with words you studied in Chapters 9–12. Write the words in the puzzle.

Across

1. Maybe it's metal, or <u>perhaps</u> plastic. I don't know.

3. The TV isn't working. Can someone f_____ it?

8. She's a good friend. I can t_____ her.

9. The dry weather will a_____ farmers in a bad way.

11. I want to buy him something s_____ for his birthday.

12. It was an o_____ day. There was nothing special about it.

Down

1. It's a p_____ party. You have to be invited.

2. Don't m_____ my trip. It's a secret.

4. Planes are made mostly of m_____.

5. Is it hard to draw the h_____ body?

6. It's not too difficult, but it's not simple, e_____.

7. He's sure he'll win. He feels very c_____.

10. G_____ is a type of metal.

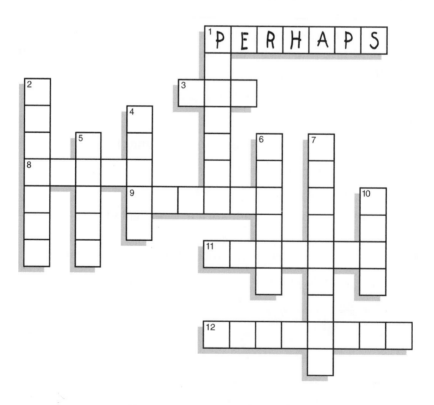

BUILDING DICTIONARY SKILLS

A Look at these dictionary entries.

> pa•tient[1] /ˈpeɪʃənt/ *n* someone who is getting medical treatment
>
> pa•tient[2] *adj* able to wait calmly for a long time or to deal with difficulties without becoming angry, anxious, or annoyed: *Try to be* **patient with** *your students.* –patiently *adv* –opposite IMPATIENT

Do you see **patient**[1] and **patient**[2]? The small, raised numbers (superscripts) tell you that the two words are different.

Complete these sentences.

1. *Patient* can be ____a noun____. It means _____.

2. *Patient* can also be _____. It means _____.

B Sometimes there is no superscript, but there is more than one meaning for a word. The meanings are numbered. Look at these dictionary entries.

> too /tu/ *adv* **1** more than is needed, wanted, or possible: *You're going too fast!* | *This is too busy a road to let the kids play near it.* ✗DON'T SAY "This is a too busy road."✗ **2** also: *Sheila wants to come too.* | *"I'm really hungry." "I am too!"* **3** very: *It shouldn't be too long until dinner's ready.*

> sweet /swit/ *adj* **1** having a taste like sugar: *Is your lemonade too sweet?* | *a sweet apple* **2** having a pleasant smell or sound: *a sweet-smelling rose* | *the sweet sounds of the cello* **3** kind, gentle, and friendly: *a sweet smile* | *a sweet little boy* **4** **have a sweet tooth** to like to eat sweet foods **5** making you feel pleased and satisfied: *Revenge is sweet!* –**sweetly** *adv* –**sweetness** *n* [U]

1. Circle *too* in each sentence, and find its definition. Write the number of the meaning.

   a. He has type A blood and I do, too. ___2___

   b. Candy is not too good for you. _____

   c. I don't like this soup. It's too salty. _____

2. Circle *sweet* in each sentence, and find its definition. Write the number of the meaning.

   a. The nurse is very sweet to all her patients. _____

   b. That little girl sings in a sweet voice. _____

   c. Some people like their coffee very sweet. _____

UNIT 4
WORKING

CHAPTER 13

Going Her Own Way

Ember Swift

GETTING READY TO READ

Talk in a small group or with the whole class.

1. The photo shows Ember Swift at work. What does she do for a living? (This question means: What's her job?)
2. Is Ember famous?
3. Would you like to have Ember's job? Why or why not?

READING

Look at the words and picture next to the reading. Then read without stopping. Don't worry about new words. Don't stop to use a dictionary. Just keep reading!

Going Her Own Way

1   Ember Swift is a singer and songwriter from Canada. She performs[1] in **clubs** all over Canada and the United States. She performs in other countries, too. Ember is very happy with her work. She says, "I'm lucky. I'm free to do what I love."

2   Ember started writing songs at **age** nine. At age ten, she started performing. She studied the piano[2] for many years. Then she learned to play the guitar. She didn't have a guitar teacher. She taught[3] **herself**. She never had singing **lessons**, either. "I learned to sing from my mother," she says.

3   Perhaps you want to know something about Ember's music. **What's it like?** Well, it's hard to **describe**. It doesn't belong to any one category such as jazz, blues, folk, or punk. It has something from each of these types of music. The words to Ember's songs can be **funny**, angry, or sad. They are often about people and relationships. Her songs are full of her feelings and ideas about the world.

4   Ember is a very **independent** young woman. She likes to decide things for herself. She wants **control** of her own life. Ember wanted control of her music **career**, too, so she didn't want to work with a big music **company**. **Instead**, she started her own company. It's called Few'll Ignite Sound. Ember's company makes her CDs and works with other **musicians**, too.

5   Making money as a musician can be difficult. Many musicians can't make enough money from their music. So they work at a **variety** of **part-time** jobs. Ember doesn't need a second job these days, but she says, "Money is sometimes a problem. There are a lot of ups and downs."[4]

6   Ember also says, "Traveling can be hard, too. All that late-night living! It's hard on your body." But she likes seeing different places. She especially likes meeting a variety of people. "It makes life interesting!"

[1] *performs* = does an act (sings, dances, etc.) for people to watch and enjoy

[2] *a piano*

[3] *taught* = past tense of *teach*

[4] *ups and downs* = good times and bad times

7 Right now Ember is working on her seventh CD. Would you like to hear some of her music? Visit her web site at www.emberswift.com.

Quick Comprehension Check

Read these sentences. Circle T (true) or F (false).

1. Ember travels to sing and play her music.   T   F

2. She writes the music and the words to her songs.   T   F

3. During the week, Ember has a job as a teacher.   T   F

4. Ember is an independent woman: she likes to decide things for herself.   T   F

5. A big music company in the United States makes Ember's CDs.   T   F

6. Most musicians have a lot of money.   T   F

EXPLORING VOCABULARY

Thinking about the Vocabulary

Which target words and phrases are new to you? Circle them here and in the reading. Then read "Going Her Own Way" again. Look at the context of each new word and phrase. Can you guess the meaning?

Target Words and Phrases			
clubs (1)	What's it like? (3)	control (4)	musicians (4)
age (2)	describe (3)	career (4)	variety (5)
herself (2)	funny (3)	company (4)	part-time (5)
lessons (2)	independent (4)	instead (4)	

Ⓐ These sentences are **about the reading**. Complete them with the words and phrases in the box.

age	clubs	describe	funny	independent
instead	part-time	What's it like	variety	

1. Ember Swift sings in _____. These are places where people go to eat, drink, dance, and listen to music.

2. Ember started writing music when she was nine years old. She started at _____ nine.

3. What kind of music does Ember play? Tell me about it. _____?

4. There's no easy way to tell someone about Ember's music. It's hard to _____.

5. The words to some of her songs make people laugh or smile. The words are _____.

6. Ember can take care of herself. She's very _____.

7. She didn't want to work for a big music company, so she started her own company _____.

8. Ember works at her music full time (forty hours a week or more). Many musicians have to find _____ jobs doing something else.

9. They work at a _____ of other jobs, such as teaching or office work.

B These sentences use the target words and phrases **in new contexts.**
Complete them with the words and phrases in the box.

age	club	described	funny	independent
instead	part-time	What's it like	variety	

1. Tell me about your new class. _____?

2. You can see a great _____ of shows on TV.

3. Jack goes to school full time and has a _____ job at the college library.

4. Dr. Adams makes his patients laugh. He tells them _____ stories.

5. We're going out for dinner, and then we're going dancing at a _____.

6. My sister didn't take my advice. She did something else _____.

7. The two drivers _____ the accident to the police in completely different ways.

8. Jimmy is only four, but he can dress himself and tie his own shoes. He's getting more _____ every day.

9. At what _____ can you get a driver's license?

C **Read these sentences. Match the boldfaced target words with their definitions.**

a. He had a long **career** as a **musician**.

b. She works for a bus **company**.

c. Drivers need to have **control** of their cars at all times.

d. I have a **lesson** with my piano teacher this afternoon.

Target Words	Definitions
1. _____	= a group of people in business together
2. _____	= a person who plays a musical instrument
3. _____	= a time used for teaching or learning something
4. _____	= the work or jobs someone does during his or her life
5. _____	= the power or ability to decide, change, or move things

Building on the Vocabulary

Studying Word Grammar

Herself is a **reflexive pronoun**. Read these sentences with *herself*:

> *Ember taught **herself** to play guitar.* = Ember taught Ember.
> *She likes to decide things for **herself**.* = Ember likes to decide things for Ember.

Study the other reflexive pronouns below.

Reflexive Pronouns

Singular	Plural
myself	ourselves
yourself	yourselves
himself	themselves
herself	
itself	

Note: *by* + reflexive pronoun = *alone*. For example: He lives by himself.

Complete these sentences with reflexive pronouns.

1. She learned to drive and got a license. Now she can drive by

   _____.

2. I like to study alone. I like to study by _____.

3. He brushed his teeth and looked at _____ in the bathroom

   mirror.

4. They didn't need help with the math. They figured out the problems
   by _____.

5. John, you seem very confident. You seem very sure
   of _____.

6. A turtle protects _____ by pulling its head and
   legs into its shell.

*a turtle inside
its shell*

DEVELOPING YOUR SKILLS

Scanning

**Read these questions about "Going Her Own Way." Scan the reading
and write short answers.**

1. What two musical instruments can Ember play? _____

2. When did she start writing songs? _____

3. Who taught her to sing? _____

4. What four types of music are mentioned in the reading? _____

   _____

5. What is Few'll Ignite Sound? _____

6. Why did Ember start her own music company? _____

   _____

7. How does Ember feel about traveling? _____

   _____

8. What's the address of Ember's website? _____

Thinking about the Main Idea

Remember: The **main idea** is the most important idea in the whole
reading. There are also **supporting facts** in a reading. They give smaller
pieces of information. They help to show the main idea.

**One of the sentences below gives the main idea of "Going Her Way."
The other two sentences are supporting facts. Read the sentences and
circle the number of the main idea. Underline the numbers of the
supporting facts.**

1. Ember Swift started to write music at age nine.
2. Ember Swift is an independent singer and songwriter.
3. Ember Swift has her own company.

Role-playing

Form a small group. One of you is a musician, and you are giving an interview. The others are newspaper reporters, and you are going to write stories about the musician. The reporters ask questions about the musician's life, and the musician answers them. For example:

REPORTER: *What kind of music do you play?*

MUSICIAN: *Rock music. I play guitar in a rock band.*

Using New Words

Work with a partner. Choose five target words or phrases from the list on page 101. On a piece of paper, use each word or phrase in a sentence.

Writing

What is something you like to do by yourself instead of with other people? Check (✔) one answer.

☐ study   ☐ watch TV   ☐ go shopping   ☐ other: _____

Give your reasons in a paragraph of four or more sentences. You can begin with: *I like to _____ by myself because . . .*

CHAPTER 14

From Play to Work

Murat Sanal beside the Bosporus in Istanbul

GETTING READY TO READ

Talk with a partner.

1. The man in the photo is from Istanbul. Where is this city?

2. Adults sometimes ask children, "What do you want to be when you grow up?"[1]

   How did you answer that question? Complete this statement:

   When I was _____ years old, I wanted to be a/an

   _____. Give your reasons.

[1] *grow up* = become an adult

READING

Look at the words and pictures next to the reading. Then read.

From Play to Work

1   When you were a child, did you **ever** play with Legos?[1] Murat Sanal did. He loved building all kinds of things from those little plastic pieces. Today, he's an architect.[2] He says, "It all began with Legos!"

2   Murat **grew up** in Turkey, in the city of Istanbul. He studied architecture at a **university** there. Then he went to another university, this one in the United States. At first, he took courses in English as a Second Language (ESL). In the ESL **program**, he met interesting people from all over the world. **Afterward**, he went on with his studies in architecture.

3   After **graduation**, Murat got his first job as an architect. He worked at a ski resort[3] in Vail, Colorado, in the United States. He went there with two friends from Istanbul. All three of them were skiers.[4] "It was a great place to work!" he says. In Vail, they could go skiing even during lunch hour. They were **serious** about their jobs, but they had a lot of fun, too.

4   Now Murat is back home in Turkey. He lives in Istanbul, near the Bosporus.[5] He walks along the water to **get to** work. His office is only ten minutes **away**, and he likes that. His job is with an architecture company. The company works on many different types of **projects**: houses, apartment buildings, resorts, and so on. Murat likes the variety of projects. He likes the people at the company, too.

5   Murat doesn't have a **regular** work **schedule**. His hours change from day to day, but he doesn't mind. Murat usually works long hours[6]—often ten hours a day. Sometimes he works more than fifty hours a week. His schedule **depends on** his projects. He says, "In this **profession**, there are lots of hours."

6   Murat likes variety in his work. He can't stand doing the same things again and again. He says, "In my job, every

continued

[1] *Legos*

[2] *architect* = a person who draws and plans buildings

[3] *resort* = a place with many hotels, often at the beach or in the mountains

[4] a *skier*

[5] *Bosporus* = the narrow waterway between the Mediterranean and the Black Sea

[6] *long hours* = work days that are longer than usual

project is a new start. It's great exercise for the mind." Murat is **proud** of his work. He's making better places for people to live, work, and play.

Quick Comprehension Check

Read these sentences. Circle T (true) or F (false).

1. Murat Sanal learned to play with Legos at a university in Turkey.   T   F
2. Murat studied architecture, and today he is an architect.   T   F
3. His first job as an architect was in Turkey.   T   F
4. Now he lives and works in Istanbul.   T   F
5. Murat says that architects work a lot of hours.   T   F
6. He doesn't care where he works.   T   F

EXPLORING VOCABULARY

Thinking about the Vocabulary

Which target words and phrases are new to you? Circle them here and in the reading. Then read "From Play To Work" again. Look at the context of each new word and phrase. Can you guess the meaning?

Target Words and Phrases			
ever (1)	afterward (2)	away (4)	depends on (5)
grew up (2)	graduation (3)	projects (4)	profession (5)
university (2)	serious (3)	regular (5)	proud (6)
program (2)	get to (4)	schedule (5)	

Using the Vocabulary

A **These sentences are about the reading. What is the meaning of each boldfaced word or phrase? Circle a, b, or c.**

1. When you were a child, did you **ever** play with Legos? *Ever* means:

   a. at any time   b. either   c. instead

2. Murat **grew up** in Turkey. His family lived in Istanbul. *Grow up* means:

   a. stay or continue   b. climb something   c. grow from a child to an adult

3. In the United States, he studied in an ESL **program**. In this sentence, *program* means:

   a. a type of company   **b.** a special group of courses   **c.** a government office

4. First, he took ESL courses. **Afterward**, he studied architecture. *Afterward* means:

   a. at a later time   **b.** perhaps   **c.** instead

5. Murat had fun skiing, but at work he was **serious**. *Serious* means:

   a. crazy   **b.** sleepy   **c.** careful

6. Murat's office is only ten minutes **away** from his house. *Away* means:

   a. at a distance   **b.** high or tall   **c.** anywhere

7. He walks along the water to **get to** his office. *Get to* means:

   a. buy something for   **b.** arrive at   **c.** figure out

8. His schedule changes. He doesn't work **regular** hours. In this sentence, *regular* means:

   a. good enough   **b.** a great variety of   **c.** happening at the same times

9. His schedule **depends on** his projects. *Depends on* means:

   a. looks forward to   **b.** changes because of   **c.** is used to

10. Murat is making better places for people to live. That makes him **proud**. *Proud* means feeling:

    a. happy about a good thing that you did   **b.** sorry about a mistake you made   **c.** nervous about your future

B These sentences use the target words and phrases **in new contexts.** Complete them with the words and phrases in the box.

afterward	away	depend on	ever	get to
grow up	program	proud	regular	serious

1. Most college students in the United States live _____ from home.

2. Where are you from? Where did you _____?

3. I sometimes forget people's names. Do you _____ do that?

4. It takes me about half an hour to _____ school in the morning.

5. He's in an MBA _____. He's taking courses in business administration.

6. I have a class at 11:00 A.M. Let's meet _____ and go to lunch.

7. He's used to working _____ hours. He works every day from 9:00 A.M. to 5:00 P.M.

8. She talks about her children all the time. She's very _____ of them.

9. Grades in school _____ several things, such as tests, papers, and work in class.

10. I'm not trying to be funny. I'm _____ about this idea.

C Read each **definition** and look at the paragraph number. Look back at the reading to find the target word for each definition. Complete the chart.

DEFINITION	PARAGRAPH	TARGET WORD
1. a place for higher education (college + graduate school)	2	_university_
2. the time when a person finishes high school or college	3	_____
3. pieces of work that take time and planning	4	_____
4. a plan of when things are going to happen	5	_____
5. work that people need a special type of education to do	5	_____

Building on the Vocabulary

Studying Word Grammar

Form the simple past tense of **regular verbs** by adding *-(e)d* to the base form of the verb (for example, work**ed**, *smil**ed***). **Irregular verbs** do not follow this rule. Some irregular verbs are *hurt, make,* and *taught.*

A In Chapters 13 and 14, you saw the **irregular verbs** *taught, had, began, grew, went, took, met,* and *was.* Write the simple past tense forms after their base forms.

Irregular Verbs			
Base Form	Simple Past Tense	Base Form	Simple Past Tense
be	*was or were*	have	
begin		meet	
go		take	
grow		teach	

B Match these simple past tense irregular verb forms with their base forms and write them in the chart: *thought, said, broke, did, made, paid, gave, spoke, built, told.*

Irregular Verbs			
Base Form	Simple Past Tense	Base Form	Simple Past Tense
break		pay	
build		say	
do		speak	
give		tell	
make		think	

DEVELOPING YOUR SKILLS

Understanding Sentences with *Because*

A Choose the best way to complete each sentence. Write the letters.

_____ 1. Murat played with Legos

_____ 2. He studied architecture in college

_____ 3. Murat likes variety in his work

_____ 4. His company gives him a lot of variety

_____ 5. His schedule often changes

_____ 6. Murat is proud of his work

a. because he wanted to be an architect.

b. because it has many different types of projects.

c. because he loved building things with them.

d. because it depends on the work he's doing.

e. because he's making better places for people to live, work, and play.

f. because he can't stand doing the same thing all the time.

B Complete this sentence. Then compare answers with a partner.

I (like/don't like) variety in my (work/classes/everyday life/food)

because _____.

Summarizing

A These seven sentences make up a summary of the reading. Number the sentences in order.

_____ a. Then he went on with his studies in the United States.

_____ b. At school in Turkey, he studied architecture.

_____ c. The company does many different types of projects.

_1_ d. As a child, Murat Sanal loved building things with Legos.

_____ e. These projects give Murat a lot of variety, and he likes that.

_____ f. After graduation, he worked as an architect at a ski resort.

_____ g. Now he works for a company in Istanbul.

B Write the sentences in Part A as a paragraph.

_____

_____

_____

_____

_____

_____

_____

Sharing Opinions

Talk about these questions in a small group. Give reasons for your opinions.

1. How many hours a week do you consider to be full-time work?
2. How does Murat feel about his long hours at work? How would you feel about working so many hours?
3. How many weeks of vacation time should a worker have in a year? Does your answer depend on the worker's type of job or number of years worked?
4. How many hours a week should full-time students spend on school work?

Using New Words

Ask and answer these questions with a partner. Then talk about your answers with the class.

1. Where did you **grow up**?
2. How long does it take you to **get to** school?
3. What is something you are **serious** about?
4. When will you finish this course? What will you do **afterward**?
5. Do you go to bed at **regular** times, or is your **schedule** different every day?

Writing

What matters most to you in a job? Check (✔) your answers. Think about why these things matter.

☐ good pay ☐ a variety of things to do ☐ a regular schedule

☐ nice people ☐ a good location (place) ☐ other: _____

Write a paragraph about your idea of a good job. You can begin with:
A good job is a job with . . .

The Honorable Judith Prakash

CHAPTER 15

Listening for the Truth

GETTING READY TO READ

Talk in a small group or with the whole class.

1. Judith Prakash is a judge. In the photo, she's wearing a judge's robes. What do judges do? Describe their work.
2. Is being a judge a good job? Why or why not?

READING

Look at the words and picture next to the reading. Then read.

Listening for the Truth

1   Judith Prakash is a **judge** in Singapore. She's a judge for the Supreme Court. It's the highest **court** in the country. Being a judge is a serious job. It's a job with a lot of **responsibility**. Judges make important **decisions**. Their decisions can change people's lives.

2   A big part of Judith's job is listening. In court, she listens and learns about **disagreements** between people. The people come to court with their **lawyers**. The lawyers speak about the case.[1] Judith was a lawyer herself for many years. The lawyers **argue** about the facts of each case. Sometimes they argue about the meaning of a **law**. Other people speak in court, too. Everyone **promises** to **tell the truth**.

3   Every case is different, so they're all interesting to Judith. She asks many questions in court. The cases give her a lot to think about. She likes this, but making a decision is never easy. She has to ask herself, "Do I have the whole story,[2] or do I need to know more?" Another important question is: Who's telling the truth? She has to figure that out. "It's the hardest part of my job," she says.

4   Things are changing in Singapore. Ten years ago, there were no women on the Supreme Court. All seventeen judges were men. Right now, there are only two women **among** the seventeen judges. However, in the lower courts,[3] almost half the judges are women. These younger women can look at Judith as a role model.[4] They can **follow** her example. Judith didn't really have any role models to follow, but she felt confident about becoming a judge. She says, "I never **doubted** that I could do the job."

5   In court, people speak to Judith with great **respect**. When she **enters** the courtroom, everyone stops talking. They all stand up. People bow[5] to her. They call her "Your Honor" to show their respect. They always listen carefully to her words. It's very different at home, she says. "I have four daughters, and they never listen!"

[1] *case* = a disagreement that must be decided in court

[2] *the whole story* = all the information about something

[3] *the lower courts* = courts below the Supreme Court

[4] *role model* = someone who other people want to be like

[5] He's *bowing.*

Quick Comprehension Check

Read these sentences. Circle T (true) or F (false).

1.	Judith Prakash is a judge for the highest court in Singapore.	T	F
2.	People bring their own judges to court.	T	F
3.	It is not easy for Judith to do her job.	T	F
4.	Judith says, "Everyone tells the truth in court."	T	F
5.	She was nervous about becoming a judge.	T	F
6.	In court, people listen carefully to Judith.	T	F

EXPLORING VOCABULARY

Thinking about the Vocabulary

Which target words and phrases are new to you? Circle them here and in the reading. Then read "Listening for the Truth" again. Look at the context of each new word and phrase. Can you guess the meaning?

Target Words and Phrases		
judge (1)	**lawyers** (2)	**among** (4)
court (1)	**argue** (2)	**follow** (4)
responsibility (1)	**law** (2)	**doubted** (4)
decisions (1)	**promises** (2)	**respect** (5)
disagreements (2)	**tell the truth** (2)	**enters** (5)

Using the Vocabulary

A These sentences are **about the reading**. Complete them with the words in the box.

among	argue	decisions	doubt	enters
follow	judge	promise	respect	responsibility

1. Judith Prakash is a _____. She makes decisions in court cases.

2. Judges have an important job. They can affect many people's lives. They have a job with a lot of _____.

3. Judges make _____ in court. They decide who is right and who is wrong.

4. A judge listens to the lawyers for both sides. The lawyers don't agree. They _____ about the facts of a case.

5. Everyone in court says, "I will tell the truth." They _____ to tell the truth.

6. Judith is one of a group of judges. There are only two women _____ the seventeen judges.

7. Years ago, there were no women judges in Singapore. As a child, Judith couldn't say, "I want to be like her." She could not _____ the example of other women.

8. Judith knew she could be a good judge. She was confident. She didn't _____ herself.

9. In court, people speak to Judith with _____. They show that they have a high opinion of her. They know she's important.

10. People stand up when a judge _____ (comes into) the courtroom.

B These sentences use the target words **in new contexts**. Complete them with the words in the box.

among	argue	decision	doubted	enter
follow	judges	promised	respect	responsibility

1. I have great _____ for Joe's opinion. We should listen to his advice.

2. You can't go in there. It says "Do not _____" on the door.

3. The teacher said, "Do Exercise A for homework. Read the directions and _____ the examples."

4. Ann's son didn't always tell the truth, but Ann always believed him. She never _____ him.

5. I need to choose a career, but I can't decide. Who can help me make the right _____?

6. There's a lot of interest in this new program _____ students at the university.

7. She hates to _____ with him, so she just says "Yes, okay, fine, anything you want."

8. Their son _____ to come home early.

9. Which film is the best? The _____ will decide on the winner.

10. They wanted to make him the president, but he didn't want so much

_____.

C Read these sentences. Match the **boldfaced** target words with their definitions.

a. Many reporters and photographers waited outside the **court**.

b. The police stopped the driver. He broke the **law** by driving too fast.

c. Some people never **tell the truth**.

d. She asked her **lawyer** for advice about selling her farm.

e. What was the cause of their **disagreement**?

Target Words	Definitions
1. _____	= give the real facts about something
2. _____	= a room where a judge listens to information about a case
3. _____	= a rule made by a government to say what people can or cannot do
4. _____	= someone who gives advice about laws or speaks for people in court
5. _____	= an argument, or a situation where people have different opinions

Building on the Vocabulary

Studying Collocations

Remember: Some words can go together, and some cannot. We can say **make** a decision but we cannot say **do** a decision. Make and do often go with different nouns.

A Underline the words after *make* or *do* in these sentences. Then complete the charts.

1. I need to **do** my homework.
2. The architect of this school **did** a good job.
3. Do you mind if I **make** a phone call?
4. I'll **do** the cooking and you **do** the dishes, okay?
5. I **made** some mistakes on the test.
6. The company often **does** business in foreign countries.
7. Don't **make** promises you can't keep.
8. Do lawyers **make** much money?
9. Who **makes** dinner at your house?

make + _____
_____
_____
_____

do + ___homework___
_____
_____
_____

B Write six sentences of your own. Use *make* or *do* + noun.

1. _____
2. _____
3. _____
4. _____
5. _____
6. _____

DEVELOPING YOUR SKILLS

Scanning

A Where is the information about these topics in "Listening for the Truth"? Scan the reading on page 115. Write the paragraph number (1–5). You will use one paragraph number twice.

___2___ **a.** what lawyers do

_____ **b.** changes in Singapore

_____ **c.** why judges' decisions are important

_____ **d.** how people talk to Judith

_____ **e.** Judith's family

_____ **f.** the hardest part of her job

B Write a sentence about each of the six topics from paragraphs 1–5. Use information from the reading.

1. _Judges' decisions can change people's lives._

2. _____

3. _____

4. _____

5. _____

6. _____

Summarizing

Use information from the reading to complete this summary.

Judith Prakash is a _____judge_____ in Singapore. She has a job
(1)

with a lot of _____. Judith has to listen to _____
(2)   (3)

between people. She has to decide who's telling the _____.
(4)

Then she has to make a _____. In _____, people
(5)   (6)

listen to her and speak to her with _____. At home, she says,
(7)

things are different!

Discussion

Talk about these questions in a small group.

1. How do you show respect for a person?
2. To whom do you show respect? Why do you show these people respect?
3. Who shows respect for you?
4. Is there anyone that everyone should respect?

Using New Words

Work with a partner. Take turns completing these statements. Then tell the class something about your partner.

1. I sometimes **argue** with _____. We **argue** about . . .
2. I need to make a **decision** about . . .
3. I **followed** _____'s example when I . . .
4. I (always/usually/rarely/never) **tell the truth** when . . .

Writing

Some people want a job with a lot of responsibility. Some people don't. What about you? Write a paragraph about your feelings. Give reasons and examples in your paragraph. You can begin with: *I (would like/wouldn't like) a job with a lot of responsibility because . . .*

CHAPTER 16

Trying to Understand

Gil Conchas in his office

GETTING READY TO READ

Talk with the whole class.

1. The man in the photo teaches at Harvard University. What do you know about Harvard?

2. What can you study at a university? Make a list of subjects, such as English, history, law, and architecture.

3. You will be reading about Gil and his brother. Who in the class has brothers? Who has sisters? Is anyone in the class an only child?[1]

[1] *an only child =* a person with no brothers or sisters

READING

Look at the words and pictures next to the reading. Then read.

Trying to Understand

1 Gil Conchas is a professor[1] at Harvard University. He teaches courses in sociology.[2] Like most professors, he also does **research**. Gil studies large groups of people. He studies the things they believe and the things they say and do. Doing research means he never stops learning.

2 Growing up, Gil didn't know much about Harvard or any other university. His family was very poor. He **was born** in the United States, but his parents were from Mexico. They didn't speak English well. They worked on farms and picked grapes, tomatoes,[3] and strawberries.[4] They also worked in **factories**. Gil's parents had a hard life, and he didn't want that for himself.

3 At age five, Gil was already a great help to his parents. He spoke English well, and he was their interpreter.[5] One time, his mother had to take a case to court, and Gil went with her. He loved helping his mother. Other **relatives** depended on him, too. "Where's Gil? We need Gil!" they said. It made him feel grown-up.[6]

4 Gil was **intelligent** and hard-working, so he became a good student. Because of his **success** in school, he had the **chance** to go to a very good university. He did well there, too. He could choose any profession.

5 Now Gil does research on poor boys and girls across the United States, especially ones who live in cities. Many of these children have serious problems. Their lives are difficult and even dangerous. Some of them—like Gil—grow up and find success as adults. Others do not. Why do some **succeed** and others **fail**? What should the government do? How can other people help? Gil is trying to find answers to these questions.

6 Gil is also writing a book about his brother, Jesse. Jesse is in **prison**. He was in a fight on the street. There was a **crowd** of about twenty young men, and one of them died. In

continued

[1] a *professor* = a teacher at a college or university

[2] *sociology* = the study of how people act in large social groups

[3] *tomatoes*

[4] a *strawberry*

[5] an *interpreter* = a person who listens to a speaker and repeats his or her words in another language

[6] *grown-up* = adult

prison, Jesse **graduated** from high school. Now he's taking college courses. Gil calls or writes to him every day and thinks about him a lot. He **compares** his brother's life with his own and **wonders**, "What made our lives so different?"

7   Gil's success makes his parents **extremely** proud. However, they don't really understand his work. Gil's father told him, "All I know is, you're doing good for other people— that's what makes me happy." His mother says, "Why is Harvard so special? Come home and teach in California! I can fix up⁷ the garage for you." Gil just smiles.

⁷ *fix up* = make nice and ready to live in

Quick Comprehension Check

Read these sentences. Circle T (true) or F (false).

1.	Gil Conchas is a student at Harvard University.	T	F
2.	His parents worked on farms and in factories.	T	F
3.	Gil wanted to do the same type of work as his parents.	T	F
4.	Today, he studies the lives of poor boys and girls in U.S. cities.	T	F
5.	Gil is also writing a book about his life.	T	F
6.	Gil lives with his parents.	T	F

EXPLORING VOCABULARY

Thinking about the Vocabulary

Which target words and phrases are new to you? Circle them here and in the reading. Then read "Trying to Understand" again. Look at the context of each new word and phrase. Can you guess the meaning?

Target Words and Phrases

research (1)	**success** (4)	**crowd** (6)
was born (2)	**chance** (4)	**graduated** (6)
factories (2)	**succeed** (5)	**compares** (6)
relatives (3)	**fail** (5)	**wonders** (6)
intelligent (4)	**prison** (6)	**extremely** (7)

Using the Vocabulary

Ⓐ Complete these sentences about the reading. What is the meaning of the **boldfaced** word or phrase? Circle a, b, or c.

1. Gil Conchas **does research** in sociology. *Do research* means:

   a. spend time talking　　**b.** read students' papers　　**c.** look for new facts

2. Gil **was born** in the United States, so he's an American. *Was born* means:

   a. arrived　　**b.** began life　　**c.** first worked

3. He helped his parents and other **relatives**, too. Relatives are:

   a. people in your family　　**b.** your friends and neighbors　　**c.** people at your job

4. Gil did well in school. He was **intelligent** and hard-working. *Intelligent* means:

   a. funny, making people laugh　　**b.** tired, needing sleep　　**c.** quick to learn and understand

5. Gil worked hard and had great **success** in school. *Success* means:

   a. a good end to what you tried to do　　**b.** a variety of problems　　**c.** projects and other things to do

6. Gil **succeeded in** building a different kind of life for himself. *Succeeded in* means:

   a. had problems with　　**b.** did very well in　　**c.** only dreamed about

7. Many boys aren't like Gil; they **fail** to make good lives for themselves. *Fail to do something* means:

   a. have fun doing it　　**b.** try to, but not do it　　**c.** be good at doing it

8. Gil **wonders**, "What made our lives so different?" *He wonders* means:

   a. He argues　　**b.** He asks himself　　**c.** He describes

9. Gil's parents are **extremely** proud of him. *Extremely* means:

   a. perhaps　　**b.** a little　　**c.** very, very

Ⓑ These sentences use the target words and phrases **in new contexts**. Complete them with the words and phrases in the box.

extremely	fail	intelligent	relatives	research
succeeded	success	were born	wonder	

1. My brother and I _____ in the same hospital.

2. Dan won't consider asking for help. He's _____ independent.

3. People respect her ideas. They say she's very _____.

4. On my grandmother's birthday, my _____ came to dinner at our house.

5. That history course is hard, but Ayako's a good student. She won't _____.

6. Those scientists are going to Antarctica to do _____.

7. I'm starting my new job on Monday. I _____ what it will be like.

8. On their second try, they _____ in climbing the mountain.

9. She's having great _____ in her acting career. She's working on her fifth movie.

C **Read these sentences. Match the boldfaced target words with their definitions.**

a. The professor said, "In your paper, describe the film and **compare** it with the book."

b. There's a big **crowd** in front of the movie theater. They're waiting to go in.

c. The judge said, "You will spend the rest of your life in **prison**."

d. **Factory** workers usually have regular work schedules.

e. I didn't have a **chance** to call her.

Target Words   **Definitions**

1. _____ = a time when you can do something

2. _____ = a place where people have to stay when they break the law

3. _____ = a place where people use machines to make products

4. _____ = look at how people or things are the same or different

5. _____ = a large group of people in one place

Building on the Vocabulary

Studying Word Grammar

When you learn a new word, try to learn its relatives—the other words in the same family. For example, the noun *success*, the verb *succeed*, and the adjective *successful* are part of the same word family. Learning these words at the same time is a good way to build your vocabulary.

A **In the reading, you saw the verb *graduate*. These sentences use this verb or another word in the same word family. <u>Underline</u> the word, and write *noun*, *verb*, or *adjective*.**

1. He's <u>graduating</u> from high school this year. _____*verb*_____

2. She's a graduate of Harvard Law School. _____

3. Graduation will be on June 2. _____

4. After college, he's going to grad school. _____

5. They're graduate students at the University of Michigan. _____

B **Complete this chart with words from Part A.**

NOUNS	VERBS	ADJECTIVES
	graduating	

DEVELOPING YOUR SKILLS

Pronoun Reference

Remember: Pronouns take the place of nouns.

What do the boldfaced pronouns mean in these sentences? Look back at the reading.

1. Paragraph 1: **He** teaches courses in sociology. _____Gill Conchas_____

2. Paragraph 2: **They** didn't speak English well. _____

3. Paragraph 3: . . . Gil went with **her**. _____

4. Paragraph 3: Other relatives depended on **him**, too. _____

5. Paragraph 5: . . . especially **ones** who live in cities. _____

6. Paragraph 6: **He** was in a fight on the street. _____

7. Paragraph 7: "All I know is, **you**'re doing good for . . . " _____

Summarizing

A These sentences make up a summary of the reading. Number the sentences in order.

_____ **a.** Now he is teaching at Harvard and doing research.

_____ **b.** His parents were from Mexico, and his family was poor.

_____ **c.** His research is about the lives of poor boys and girls in the United States.

__1__ **d.** Gil Conchas was born in California.

_____ **e.** He is also writing a book.

_____ **f.** He helped them by speaking English for them.

_____ **g.** He worked hard in school, did well, and went to a good university.

_____ **h.** It is about his brother in prison.

B Write the eight sentences in Part A as a paragraph.

_____

_____

_____

_____

_____

_____

_____

_____

_____

_____

_____

Sharing Opinions

What does success mean to you? Circle your answers to the questions below. Then talk with a partner. Find out what he or she thinks and why.

1 = extremely important   2 = important   3 = not very important
4 = it doesn't matter

How important is . . .	Your Answers	Your Partner's Answers
1. being famous?	1 2 3 4	1 2 3 4
2. making a lot of money?	1 2 3 4	1 2 3 4
3. being free and independent?	1 2 3 4	1 2 3 4
4. being married and having children?	1 2 3 4	1 2 3 4
5. having a job with a lot of responsibility?	1 2 3 4	1 2 3 4
6. having the respect of other people?	1 2 3 4	1 2 3 4

Using New Words

Work with a partner. Choose five target words or phrases from the list on page 124. On a piece of paper, use each word or phrase in a sentence.

Writing

Write a paragraph comparing yourself to a brother or sister or another relative. Write about ways you are different or ways you are alike. You can begin with:
My (older sister, mother, brother) and I are (very different/a lot alike).

You can use sentences like:

My sister always _____, but I _____.

My father likes to _____, but I _____.

We both _____.

Wrap-up

REVIEWING VOCABULARY

A Fill in the circles and complete the sentence. Use the three correct words from the box.

| club | judge | lawyer | musician | profession | relative | research |

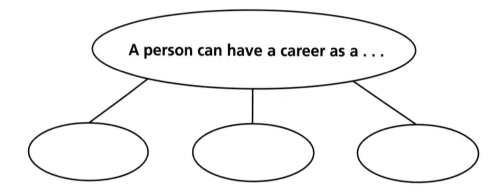

A person can have a career as a . . .

B Match the words with their definitions. Write the letter.

_____ 1. a company

_____ 2. a decision

_____ 3. a crowd

_____ 4. a disagreement

_____ 5. a factory

_____ 6. a law

_____ 7. the truth

a. a rule that all of the people of a state or country have to follow

b. a large group of people together in a place

c. a group of people doing business

d. the correct facts about something

e. something that a person decides or makes up his or her mind about

f. an argument between people with different opinions

g. a place where people use machines to make things in large numbers

C Complete these sentences with the words and phrases in the box. There is one extra word.

age	compares	describe	doubt	failed	followed
funny	get to	grow up	intelligent	was born	

1. The baby _____ at the hospital in the middle of the night.

2. The adults asked the girl, "What do you want to do when you _____?"

3. How long does it take you to _____ school in the morning?

4. He always _____ his life here to his life back home.

5. How would you _____ the taste of Turkish coffee? What's it like?

6. He _____ his brother's example and became a lawyer.

7. She believes that she can keep her plan a secret, but I _____ it.

8. They told us a _____ story. We all laughed.

9. The test was extremely hard, and several students _____ it.

10. Do you think it's okay to ask a woman her _____?

EXPANDING VOCABULARY

A **Suffixes** come at the ends of words. They can tell you something about word meanings. For example, the suffix -er or -or is often found in words for people. It can mean a person who does something, as in *traveler* or *collector*.

Complete these sentences with *advisor, dreamer, neighbor,* and *researcher*.

1. That scientist is a _____ at a big plastics company.

2. I need to see my _____ for advice on choosing courses for next year.

3. I can't stand my _____. He makes too much noise and wakes me up at night.

4. He talks about all his great plans, but he never does anything. He's just a _____.

B Certain **prepositions** (such as *to, on,* and *at*) often follow certain verbs. For example, you will often see *wait + for, belong + to,* and *think + about.*

Complete the sentences below. Write verbs + prepositions.

VERB	PREPOSITION	OBJECT
argue	about	something
depend	on	something or someone
succeed	in	doing something
wonder	about	something or someone

1. Small children ____*depend on*____ their parents. They need them.
2. Those two disagree all the time. They _____ everything!
3. I sometimes _____ my old friends from school. Where are they now?
4. Will they _____ protecting the animals of the Galápagos?
5. We'll leave some time between 9:00 A.M. and 10:00 A.M. It will _____ the bus schedule.

C Write a sentence with each verb + preposition from Part B.

1. _____
2. _____
3. _____
4. _____

PLAYING WITH WORDS

There are ten target words from Unit 4 in this puzzle. The words go across (→) and down (↓). Find the words and circle them. Then use the words to complete the sentences below.

```
W  X (A  W  A  Y) Y  X  F  E
I  N  S  T  E  A  D  Z  P  X
D  F  Z  D  W  W  N  B  R  T
M  H  P  W  H  X  E  V  E  R
K  W  R  V  A  M  O  N  G  E
P  R  O  J  E  C  T  T  U  M
W  Q  U  B  H  R  X  V  L  E
Z  X  D  T  Q  N  J  X  A  L
F  P  R  O  M  I  S  E  R  Y
G  R  A  D  U  A  T  I  O  N
```

1. We can walk to the library from here. It's only five minutes
   _____away_____.

2. Please _____ me that you'll call me later!

3. The patient's heartbeat was slow and _____.

4. Do you _____ wonder what it's like to be rich and famous?

5. He'll finish school in May. _____ is on May 20.

6. The boys are working on a _____ for their science class.

7. He wants to make his parents _____ of him.

8. He didn't drive to work today. He took the bus _____.

9. Are there good relationships _____ all the players on the team?

10. He didn't get hurt in the accident. He was _____ lucky.

BUILDING DICTIONARY SKILLS

A Look at these dictionary entries.

> **pro•gram**[1] /ˈproʊɡræm, -ɡrəm/ *n* **1** a show on television or radio: *There's a program about whales on channel 9.* **2** a set of instructions given to a computer to make it do a particular job: *a software program that helps you with household finances* **3** a set of planned activities with a specific purpose: *Stanford's MBA program | a government program to house the homeless | Lucy's exercise program includes weight lifting and swimming.* **4** a printed description of what will happen at a play, concert etc. and of the people who will be performing . . .
>
> **pro•gram**[2] *v* **-mmed, -mming** [T] **1** to set a machine to operate in a particular way: *I've programmed the VCR to record that movie you wanted.* **2** to give a set of instructions to a computer to make it do a particular job.

Now look at the uses of *program* in these sentences. Write *noun* or *verb* on the line followed by the number of the meaning.

1. You can read the actors' names in the program. <u> noun </u> <u> 4 </u>

2. There's a program about the Olympics on TV. <u>   </u> <u>   </u>

3. Can you program my VCR for me? <u>   </u> <u>   </u>

4. She's in a graduate program in business. <u>   </u> <u>   </u>

5. He writes programs for computer games. <u>   </u> <u>   </u>

B Dictionaries sometimes show verb forms. Look at the entry for program.[2]

- **-mmed** means the simple past tense form is *programmed*
- **-mming** means the *–ing* form is *programming*

The verb *program* is **regular** (the simple past ends in *–ed*). Dictionaries don't usually show the *–ed* form. In this case, however, there is a spelling change *(program + m + ed)*, so the dictionary shows it. The dictionary always shows **irregular** verb forms (such as *go, went, gone*).

> **bend**[1] /bɛnd/ *v* **bent, bent, bending** [I, T] **1** to move a part of your body so that it is no longer straight . . .

> **de•scribe** /dɪˈskraɪb/ *v* [T] to say what someone or something is like by giving details: *Can you describe the man?* . . .

1. **a.** Look at the first part of the entry for the word *bend*. Is it a regular or an irregular verb? _____

   b. What is the simple past tense form? _____

2. **a.** Look at the entry for the word *describe*. Is it a regular or an irregular verb? _____

   b. What is the simple past tense form? _____

Vocabulary Self-Test 1

Circle the letter of the word or phrase that best completes each sentence.

Example:

I almost never see my friends these days, and I _____ them.

a. count   **c.** miss
b. grow up   d. find out

1. I have a cold, so it's hard to _____ through my nose.
   a. argue   c. breathe
   b. shine   d. paint

2. I need to _____ the answer to this math problem.
   a. go on   c. belong to
   b. figure out   d. look forward to

3. You should ask your doctor questions about your _____.
   a. health   c. government
   b. roof   d. island

4. Think about it before you make a _____.
   a. finger   c. decision
   b. dream   d. size

5. She had a bad car _____, but she's fine.
   a. truth   c. sight
   b. neighbor   d. accident

6. He _____ books about music. He has more than 100.
   a. climbs   c. fixes
   b. invites   d. collects

7. The story was true. _____, nobody believed it.
   a. Instead   c. However
   b. Especially   d. Of course

8. She made a birthday cake in the _____ of a heart.
   a. control   c. feeling
   b. shape   d. record

9. Those students are new here, so they're not _____ the weather.
   a. used to
   b. proud of
   c. nervous about
   d. kind to

10. Antarctica looks small on this map, but it's _____ bigger than Australia.
    a. yet
    b. several
    c. either
    d. actually

11. That was really easy. I just _____ the directions on the box.
    a. followed
    b. imagined
    c. bent
    d. received

12. Some rich people have their own _____ planes.
    a. sweet
    b. confident
    c. private
    d. stone

13. He doesn't care about clothes. Clothes don't _____ to him.
    a. matter
    b. consider
    c. mind
    d. fail

14. Texas is a big state, but Alaska is _____ bigger.
    a. away
    b. even
    c. such as
    d. each other

15. It's always warm there. The temperature never goes _____ 60°F.
    a. below
    b. among
    c. during
    d. along

16. I can't wear this hat. It's _____ small for me.
    a. ever
    b. twice
    c. perhaps
    d. too

17. It's _____ to walk alone in this city at night. Don't do it.
    a. ordinary
    b. dangerous
    c. special
    d. busy

18. Those two kinds of chocolate are good, but this one is the _____.
    a. regular
    b. simple
    c. best
    d. whole

19. You should keep your money in a _____ place.
    a. crazy
    b. safe
    c. cool
    d. tiny

20. What _____ of car does he drive?
    a. secret
    c. mountain
    b. middle
    d. type

21. People can go to libraries to find _____ about almost anything.
    a. nurses
    c. shoulders
    b. facts
    d. wings

22. People often use dictionaries to _____ the meanings of new words.
    a. look up
    c. describe
    b. make up
    d. protect

23. I have great _____ for your mother and father.
    a. age
    c. snow
    b. bone
    d. respect

24. He talked about two of his friends, but he didn't _____ their names.
    a. travel
    c. hurt
    b. mention
    d. draw

25. Take my _____ and don't eat at that restaurant.
    a. adult
    c. advice
    b. education
    d. mind

26. Children need _____. They should go out and play.
    a. brain
    c. metal
    b. career
    d. exercise

27. Eggs, milk, and cheese are just a few of the _____ of their farm.
    a. companies
    c. products
    b. patients
    d. teams

28. Why did he color his hair blue? What was his _____ for doing that?
    a. reason
    c. rock
    b. land
    d. parent

29. We were afraid it was going to rain. _____, it didn't.
    a. Luckily
    c. Only
    b. Completely
    d. Exactly

30. Everyone studies the _____ of their country in school.
    a. distance
    b. history
    c. judge
    d. graduation

31. Who will _____ the baby?
    a. climb
    b. depend on
    c. take care of
    d. taste

32. College students usually have to do _____.
    a. disagreement
    b. court
    c. factory
    d. research

See the Answer Key on page 246.

Songkran

Celebrating Songkran in Bangkok

GETTING READY TO READ

Talk with a partner.

1. What do you see in the photo?
2. Do you celebrate the start of a new year? When does the new year begin? What do you do?
3. What other New Year celebrations do you know about? Make a list.

READING

Look at the words and pictures next to the reading. Then read without stopping. Don't worry about new words. Don't stop to use a dictionary. Just keep reading!

Songkran

1   In many parts of the world, a new year begins on the first of January. However, new year **celebrations** also happen at other times. The start of a new year depends on the traditions of a country, a **culture**, or a religion.[1] There is also great variety in the ways people **celebrate**. Some people go to **church**, eat special foods, or throw a party.[2] In Thailand, people celebrate the new year in April, and they do it with water.

2   The month of April is extremely hot in Thailand. Maybe that is why water is important in the Thai new year celebration. Water helps people feel cool, clean, and **fresh**, and the new year is a time for a fresh start (a new beginning).

3   The name of the Thai New Year's celebration is *Songkran*. This **holiday** begins in the middle of April (the day depends on the **moon**), and it **lasts** for several days. People look forward to it, especially children. They get ready for Songkran by collecting water **guns**, buckets,[3] and hoses.[4] They want these things because during Songkran, they **throw** water at people. Children get each other completely **wet**. They throw water at adults, too. If you want to stay **dry**, you have to stay inside. Everybody who goes outside gets wet!

4   Jad Kanchanalak grew up in Thailand. She remembers all the fun of Songkran. She says, "We always played outside in front of our house in Bangkok. I **used to** get wet and stay wet all day! Nobody really minded getting wet. Everyone **expected** it. It was part of the holiday fun."

5   Songkran has more serious traditions, too. For example, people make visits to temples,[5] and many people visit older relatives. They go to see them to show respect. The older

continued

[1] a *religion* = a set of beliefs in one or more gods. Christianity and Islam are religions.

[2] *throw a party* = plan and have a party

[3] a *bucket*

[4] a *hose*

[5] a Buddhist *temple*

people **pour** water over the hands of the younger ones, and they wish them good luck in the coming year. The water has flowers in it and smells very nice.

6   Jad remembers, "We used to make one or two visits to relatives. Then my sisters and I were free to play. Songkran is a very happy time."

Quick Comprehension Check

Read these sentences. Circle T (true) or F (false).

1.	Everyone around the world celebrates the new year on the same day.	T	F
2.	People in Thailand celebrate Songkran in the middle of April.	T	F
3.	The weather in Thailand is cool in April.	T	F
4.	Thai children celebrate the new year by throwing water at people.	T	F
5.	Songkran has some serious traditions.	T	F
6.	Older people show respect to younger people on Songkran.	T	F

EXPLORING VOCABULARY

Thinking about the Vocabulary

Which target words and phrases are new to you? Circle them here and in the reading. Then read "Songkran" again. Look at the context of each new word and phrase. Can you guess the meaning?

Target Words and Phrases		
celebrations (1)	holiday (3)	wet (3)
culture (1)	moon (3)	dry (3)
celebrate (1)	lasts (3)	used to (4)
church (1)	guns (3)	expected (4)
fresh (2)	throw (3)	pour (5)

A Label these pictures. Write *a church, a water gun, the moon, dry,* and *wet.*

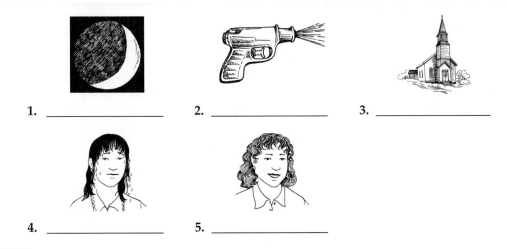

1. _____   2. _____   3. _____

4. _____   5. _____

B These sentences are **about the reading.** Complete them with the words and phrases in the box.

celebration	celebrate	cultures	expect	fresh
holiday	lasts	pour	throw	used to

1. In many countries, a New Year's _____ happens on the evening of December 31. It's a happy time. People often go to parties.

2. In Thailand, people _____ the New Year in April. They don't work. They have fun.

3. New year celebrations are not the same in all _____ (groups with their own traditions, ideas, art, music, and so on).

4. When you are hot, dirty, or tired, water helps you feel cool, clean, and _____.

5. Songkran is a _____. Schools and businesses are usually closed on these days.

6. Songkran doesn't end after just one day. This holiday _____ for several days.

7. Children use cups and buckets to _____ water at each other.

8. Everyone knows that they will get wet. They _____ to get wet.

9. Jad Kanchanalak always loved Songkran. It was always hot, and she
_____ stay wet all day.

10. Jad's older relatives used to _____ water over her hands. They
made the water pass over her hands.

C These sentences use the target words and phrases **in new contexts.**
Complete them with the words and phrases in the box.

celebrations	celebrate	culture	expect	fresh
holiday	lasts	poured	throws	used to

1. It's good for your health to eat a lot of _____ vegetables.

2. The pitcher _____ the baseball, and the batter tries to hit it.

3. I _____ take guitar lessons, but I stopped last year.

4. She _____ some more coffee into my cup.

5. That TV program comes on at 8:00 and _____ one hour.

6. Slava thought he would get to class on time. He didn't _____
to be late.

7. Jiselle is in Moscow. She's learning about Russian _____: how
the people of Russia think and act, what they believe, etc.

8. Independence Day is an important _____ in the United States.

9. Americans _____ Independence Day on July 4.

10. Independence Day is the "birthday" of the United States. Americans have
_____ in many cities.

Building on the Vocabulary

Studying Word Grammar

In Unit 3, you practiced *be used to* + noun/pronoun. When you're used to
something, it isn't new or strange or difficult for you. For example:

> The nurse didn't mind the sight of blood. She **was used to** it.
> I'm working nights now, and it's hard. I'**m not used to** this schedule.

Used to + base verb has a different meaning. It shows an action that happened
regularly in the past but doesn't happen now:

> He **used to smoke**. (He stopped smoking. He doesn't smoke anymore.)
> She **used to have** a Toyota. Then she sold it. Now she has a Honda.

Write these sentences in a different way. Use *be used to* or *used to* + base verb.

1. She stopped going to that school.   <u>She used to go to that school.</u>
2. I always watch American movies.   <u>I'm used to American movies.</u>
3. He stopped working part-time. _____
4. We always have hot weather. _____
5. I always work on one type of computer. _____
6. You stopped giving me advice. _____

DEVELOPING YOUR SKILLS

Reading for Details

Read these sentences. Then reread "Songkran" for the answers. If the reading doesn't give the information, check (✔) *It doesn't say.*

	YES	NO	IT DOESN'T SAY.
1. Songkran is the name for the Thai new year celebration.	✔		
2. The new year begins on January 1 in Thailand.			
3. The weather in Thailand is always hot.			
4. Songkran lasts for several weeks.			
5. Thai children look forward to this holiday.			
6. Jad used to play outside and stay wet all day.			
7. Thai schools are closed during Songkran.			
8. Adults never throw water at each other during Songkran.			
9. People traditionally visit relatives at Songkran.			
10. Songkran is Thailand's most important holiday.			

Summarizing

Use information from the reading to complete this summary.

People in _____ celebrate the start of _____ in
             (1)   (2)

April. The name of the Thai new year celebration is _____. Thai
                                                              (3)

people celebrate the holiday with _____. Children
                                          (4)

_____ it at people. Families visit their _____ during
       (5)   (6)

Songkran.

Interviewing

**Read the questions in the chart. Write your answers. Then interview a
partner. Write your partner's answers.**

	YOU	YOUR PARTNER
1. What was your favorite holiday when you were a child?		
2. What did you use to do on this holiday?		
3. What holidays do you celebrate now?		

Using New Words

**Work with a partner. Take turns asking for and giving information. Then
tell the class something about your partner.**

1. Name a **fresh** fruit that tastes good.
2. Name something you should keep **dry**.
3. Tell when you like and don't like to get **wet**.
4. Name something you can **throw** and something you can't.
5. Tell something you **expect** to do, and tell when you **expect** to do it.

Writing

**Write about a holiday that you used to enjoy as a child. Describe your
holiday traditions. What did you use to do? You can begin with: *When I was
a child, my favorite holiday was* _____. *I / My family used to . . .***

CHAPTER 18

Québec's Winter Carnival

Inside the Ice Hotel

GETTING READY TO READ

Talk with a partner.

1. Which is more of a problem for you, being too hot or being too cold? Why?

2. In cold weather, do you like to be inside or outside? What do you enjoy doing in cold weather?

3. Can you label these pictures of winter sports? Write *skiing, skating,* or *dogsled racing* under each picture.

a. _____

b. _____

c. _____

147

READING

Look at the words and pictures next to the reading. Then read.

Québec's Winter Carnival

1   Winters in the city of Québec, Canada, are very cold. There is ice and snow all around. The days are short and the nights are long. It doesn't seem like much fun, does it? But the city is beautiful in the snow. For the people of Québec, it's the **perfect** time to celebrate. So they have a big party. It's the Québec Winter Carnival, and it's the largest winter **festival** in the world. It lasts for three weeks.

2   There are lots of things to do at Carnival. You can walk around the city and see the fine stone buildings and the beautiful churches. You can watch dogsled races through the **narrow** streets. There are also canoe[1] races on the **wide** Saint Lawrence River. If you get cold, choose one of Québec's **excellent** restaurants and have a good hot **meal**.

1 a canoe

3   Outside the city, you can go skiing or skating, or you can try to climb a wall of ice. You can even drive a dogsled yourself. At night, you'll **be able to** watch fireworks.[2] Then afterwards, you can go to sleep in a hotel made of ice!

2 fireworks

4   Yes, it's true. Outside the city, there is a hotel completely made of ice and snow. The Ice Hotel opens for business in January. It stays open for about three months. Its walls of ice are several feet **thick**. There is a bar inside the hotel with tables and chairs made of ice. Ten-year-old Bobby visited the bar with his father, and they **ordered** a **couple** of soft drinks. Their drinks came in glasses made of ice. **While** he was there, Bobby used one of the computers in the bar to send e-mail to his friends and relatives. People can even send photos of themselves at the Ice Hotel.

3 *Deerskins* come from deer.

5   Perhaps you are wondering about the beds in this hotel. The beds are all made of ice, too. They have deerskins[3] on top. The rooms are only about 25°F (-5°C), so the hotel gives each **guest** a warm sleeping bag.[4] Bobby and his father had to wear their hats to bed, too.

4 a *sleeping bag*

6   Maybe you'd like the chance to stay at the Ice Hotel. Does it seem to you like an interesting **experience**? Hundreds of guests stay there each year, but almost no one stays a second night. Maybe you **would rather** stay at a **regular** hotel, with a fine restaurant and nice warm beds. Either way,[5] beautiful Québec has something for everyone during Carnival.

[5] *either way* = It doesn't matter which one

Quick Comprehension Check

Read these sentences. Circle T (true) or F (false).

1. Québec is a beautiful city in Canada.	T	F
2. Winter is very cold in Québec.	T	F
3. Québec's Winter Carnival lasts for three months.	T	F
4. There are many things to do in and outside the city.	T	F
5. People can stay at a hotel made of ice.	T	F
6. The hotel has ordinary beds, tables, and chairs.	T	F

EXPLORING VOCABULARY

Thinking about the Vocabulary

Which target words and phrases are new to you? Circle them here and in the reading. Then read "Quebec's Winter Carnival" again. Look at the context of each new word and phrase. Can you guess the meaning?

Target Words and Phrases

perfect (1)	**meal** (2)	**while** (4)
festival (1)	**be able to** (3)	**guest** (5)
narrow (2)	**thick** (4)	**experience** (6)
wide (2)	**ordered** (4)	**would rather** (6)
excellent (2)	**couple** (4)	**regular** (6)

Using the Vocabulary

A These sentences are about the reading. What is the meaning of each **boldfaced** word or phrase? Circle a, b, or c.

1. Winter Carnival in Québec is the world's largest winter **festival**. A festival is:

   a. a celebration   **b.** a type of sport   **c.** a time of bad weather

2. The streets of Québec are **narrow**, so they can be a problem for buses and big trucks. *Narrow* means:

   a. nice and clean   **b.** very old   **c.** not big across

3. Québec has **excellent** restaurants, so visitors can eat well. *Excellent* means:

   a. dangerous   **b.** too expensive   **c.** extremely good

4. On cold days, people want hot **meals**. They can get them in restaurants. A meal is:

   a. something to wear   **b.** something to eat   **c.** something to listen to

5. People at Carnival **are able to** see fireworks at night. *Are able to* means:

   a. can   **b.** have to   **c.** never

6. Bobby and his father **ordered** soft drinks at the hotel. In this sentence, *ordered* means:

   a. poured   **b.** asked a waiter for   **c.** argued about

7. They got **a couple of** drinks. *A couple of* means:

   a. two   **b.** ten   **c.** many

8. The Ice Hotel has warm sleeping bags for its **guests**. Its guests are:

   a. its prisoners   **b.** its musicians   **c.** its visitors

9. Most hotels aren't made of ice, but the Ice Hotel isn't a **regular** hotel. In this sentence, *regular* means:

   a. usual, ordinary   **b.** independent   **c.** famous

10. Some people would like to stay at the Ice Hotel. Others **would rather** stay at another hotel. *Would rather* means:

    a. would hate to   **b.** would like it better to   **c.** would never

B These sentences use the target words and phrases **in new contexts.** Complete them with the words and phrases in the box.

be able to	a couple of	excellent	festival	guests
I'd rather	meals	narrow	order	regular

1. I like my _____ at regular hours: breakfast at 7:00 A.M., lunch at noon, and dinner at 6:00 P.M.

2. Don't worry. You made an _____ decision. There's no doubt about it.

3. Each student can invite four people to graduation. That's right—only four _____ per student.

4. There is a famous film _____ at Cannes in France. People go there to see many new movies.

5. He can't fail any more courses. If he fails another, he won't _____ graduate.

6. This restaurant has a great variety of good food. It's hard to decide what to _____!

7. These shoes hurt my feet. They're too _____.

8. I'm sorry to keep you waiting. I'll be ready in _____ minutes.

9. Let's not go to the movies. _____ stay home and watch a video.

10. He's too tall to buy clothes in a _____ store. He has to order specially made clothes.

C **Read these sentences. Match the boldfaced target words with their definitions.**

a. You should be a lawyer. That's the **perfect** profession for you. You love to argue!

b. **While** we were at the beach, we saw some unusual birds.

c. I didn't like my job in the factory. Working there wasn't a good **experience** for me.

d. The building has **thick** walls, so it's quiet inside.

e. It's a **wide** lake. It's more than 100 miles across.

Target Words   **Definitions**

1. _____ = large across, not narrow (*a . . . street/river*)

2. _____ = something that happens to a person

3. _____ = exactly right, the best

4. _____ = large between its two sides, not thin (*. . . ice/books*)

5. _____ = during the time that, when

Building on the Vocabulary

Studying Collocations

Adjectives such as *thick, wide, long, tall*, and *high* can follow measure words (such as *inches, feet,* or *miles*) to tell how big something or someone is. For example:

> The river is about *a mile* **wide**.
> He is *six feet, two inches* **tall**.
> Our apartment building is *six stories* **high**.

Write your answers to these questions. Use number + measure word + *thick/wide/tall/long/high.*

1. How thick is your dictionary? _____ It's two inches thick. _____

2. How high is the building you live in? _____

3. How tall are you? _____

4. How long is your hair? _____

5. How wide is the room you are in? _____

DEVELOPING YOUR SKILLS

Scanning

A **Where is the information about these topics in "Québec's Winter Carnival"? Scan the reading on pages 148–149. Write the paragraph number (1–6).**

_____ **a.** the Ice Hotel   _____ **d.** in the city during Carnival

_1_ **b.** Québec in the winter   _____ **e.** things to do outside the city

_____ **c.** choosing a hotel   _____ **f.** beds at the Ice Hotel

B **Write a sentence about each of the six topics from paragraphs 1–6. Use information from the reading.**

1. _____

2. _____

3. _____

4. _____

5. _____

6. _____

Thinking about the Main Idea

Complete this statement to tell the main idea of the reading.

There are many _____ things to do at Québec's Winter Carnival, such as _____

_____.

Discussion

Talk about these questions with a partner or in a small group. Then share your answers with the class.

1. Would you like to go to Québec in the winter, or would you rather go somewhere warm?
2. Would you like to be a guest at the Ice Hotel?
3. Would you rather go skiing or dogsled racing?
4. What other festivals do you know about?

Using New Words

Work with a partner. Choose five target words or phrases from the list on page 149. On a piece of paper, use each word or phrase in a sentence.

Writing

Imagine the perfect restaurant meal. Complete the following statements. Then write a paragraph.

1. The perfect meal for me would be at _____. (Where would you eat?)
2. _____ would be my guests. (Who would be with you?)
3. First, we would eat _____. Then we would have _____. (What would you eat?)
4. We would drink _____. (What would you drink?)
5. While we were eating, we would listen to _____. (What kind of music would you listen to?)
6. After the meal, I would _____. (What would you do afterward?)

CHAPTER 19

Celebrating a New Baby

A proud father

GETTING READY TO READ

Talk with a partner.

1. What do you see in the photo?
2. Did you ever celebrate the birth of a new baby? Who was the baby? What did you do to celebrate?
3. Who gave you your name? Why did they choose it? Does your name have a special meaning?

READING

Look at the words and pictures next to the reading. Then read.

Celebrating a New Baby

1   What did your parents do to celebrate when you were born? Of course you can't remember, but maybe they have photos from a ceremony[1] of some kind. People usually have ceremonies to **mark** important **events** in life. For example, there are **wedding** ceremonies. Getting married is an important event, and having a baby is, too. In most cultures, there are ceremonies and other **traditional** ways to celebrate a new child in the family.

2   In the United States, the proud parents of a new baby often decorate[2] their front door. It's an **exciting** time for them, and they want to **share** the good **news** with their neighbors. For example, they may put balloons[3] on their door. Pink balloons mean the baby is a girl. Blue ones are for boys. New fathers used to **hand out** cigars[4] to all their friends. Today, that tradition continues, but things are a little different. Only about 25% of American adults smoke now, so the cigars are sometimes made of chocolate.

3   People around the world often celebrate a new baby with some type of ceremony, perhaps a **religious** ceremony. This may **take place** when a baby is a few days or weeks old. In Korea, there's a traditional ceremony on the baby's 100th day. In Mexico, many new parents dress their babies in special clothes and take them to church. In some African cultures, the family **plants** a tree.

4   New babies in every culture **have one thing in common:** they all need names. Sometimes the parents choose their baby's name before the child is born. However, a baby's name is not always the parents' decision. Sometimes the name depends on family traditions, and some babies get their names at religious ceremonies.

5   Parents in the United States sometimes put the news about their baby in the newspaper. For example:

Smith, Michael James, Jr.[5] Born July 4, son of Michael J. and Sarah Dean Smith of Deerfield.

continued

[1] a *ceremony* = a formal group of actions and words used at a special time

[2] *decorate* = make a thing or a place look nice

[3] *balloons*

[4] a *cigar*

[5] *Jr.* = (the abbreviation for) *Junior,* used for a son with the same name as his father

This baby has the same name as his father. *Michael* is a very **common** American name. Other American parents want unusual names for their children. Apple Kaufmann has a very uncommon first name. She says, "My parents **let** my eight-year-old brother name me!"

6   The parents of new babies often receive presents. In the United States, friends send them **cards**, flowers, and baby clothes. Presents, celebrations—these things are great. But what do most new parents really need? More sleep!

Quick Comprehension Check

Read these sentences. Circle T (true) or F (false).

1. New parents in the United States usually decorate their cars.   T   F

2. Americans give cigars to new babies.   T   F

3. The time for a ceremony for a new baby depends on the culture.   T   F

4. Planting a tree to celebrate a new baby is an American tradition.   T   F

5. Boys in the United States never have the same name as their father.   T   F

6. In the United States, people often give presents to new parents.   T   F

EXPLORING VOCABULARY

Thinking about the Vocabulary

Which target words and phrases are new to you? Circle them here and in the reading. Then read "Celebrating a New Baby" again. Look at the context of each new word and phrase. Can you guess the meaning?

Target Words and Phrases

mark (1)	share (2)	plants (3)
events (1)	news (2)	**have one thing in common** (4)
wedding (1)	hand out (2)	common (5)
traditional (1)	religious (3)	let (5)
exciting (2)	take place (3)	cards (6)

Using the Vocabulary

A These words are **about the reading**. Complete them with the words and phrases in the box.

exciting	hand out	have something in common	let	mark
news	religious	takes place		traditional	wedding

1. People want to _____ or celebrate important events in their lives, such as having a baby.

2. A _____ is an important event. It is the ceremony when two people get married.

3. Most cultures have _____ ways to celebrate a new baby. People in that culture do the same things—year after year, baby after baby.

4. Having a baby is an _____ event. It makes people feel happy. It makes them look forward to the future.

5. New parents in the United States sometimes put blue balloons on the front of their house or apartment. The balloons tell people the _____: "The baby is a boy!"

6. New fathers used to _____ cigars to their friends. Today, they sometimes give friends cigars made of chocolate.

7. There is a ceremony for babies in Korea. It _____ on the 100th day of the baby's life. (It happens on that day.)

8. Some people have a _____ ceremony for a new baby in a church or temple.

9. All new babies need names, so all new babies _____.

10. Ms. Kaufmann's brother wanted to name the new baby, and his parents said, "OK, you can do it." They _____ him name her Apple.

B These sentences use the target words and phrases **in new contexts**. Complete them with the words and phrases in the box.

exciting	handed out	have something in common	let	mark
news	religious	took place		traditional	wedding

1. They got married last Saturday. There were 100 guests at the _____ and at the reception afterward.

2. The teacher _____ a couple of papers to each student.

3. I have some good _____: I got the job!

4. You and I share the same birthday. We _____.

5. Most Americans think of nine-to-five as the _____ work schedule.

6. Does the government of your country _____ all adults own guns?

7. This newspaper started 200 years ago. Next week, they will _____ their 200th anniversary.

8. The whole family belongs to the same church and shares the same _____ beliefs.

9. The first Olympic Games _____ in Greece.

10. Would you like to travel to the moon? It would be an _____ experience!

C **Read these sentences. Match the boldfaced target words with their definitions.**

a. Carmen and her neighbor **share** the same birthday: February 29. It's not a **common** birthday.

b. People in the United States often send **cards** to friends on their birthdays.

c. In the spring, I **plant** flowers and vegetables in my garden.

d. People can learn about world **events** by reading the newspaper.

Target Words   **Definitions**

1. _____ = usual; easy to find because there are many

2. _____ = put something into the ground so that it can grow

3. _____ = things that happen, especially important things

4. _____ = pieces of folded paper with pictures and messages on them

5. _____ = have the same thing as someone else

Building on the Vocabulary

Studying Word Grammar

Quantifiers are words that tell how many or how much.

- Use the following quantifiers with noncount nouns:
  much, a lot of, enough, some, any, a little, and *no.*

    We need **a little** sugar for our tea.

- Use *any* and *much* only with negative verbs or in questions; for example:

    We don't have **much** time. Is there **any** snow?

- Don't use a negative verb with the quantifier *no:* They ~~don't~~ have **no** money.

Write six sentences. In each sentence, use a quantifier + noncount noun. Choose from these nouns: *advice, blood, exercise, fun, gold, ice, luck, news, plastic, respect, success.*

1. _____

2. _____

3. _____

4. _____

5. _____

6. _____

DEVELOPING YOUR SKILLS

Understanding Sentences with *Because*

A **Choose the best way to complete each sentence.**

_____ 1. Some new parents decorate their front door

_____ 2. Some new fathers hand out cigars

_____ 3. Some families have a tree-planting ceremony

_____ 4. Some American boys' names end in *Jr.*

_____ 5. Ms. Kaufmann has the unusual name Apple

_____ 6. People around the world celebrate having a baby

a. because it's a tradition in some African cultures.

b. because her brother chose that name.

c. because they want to share the news about their baby.

d. because it's an American tradition.

e. because it's a big event in their lives.

f. because they share a name with their father.

B Complete this sentence. Then compare answers with a partner.

I (like/don't like) my name because _____.

Summarizing

Write answers to these questions on a piece of paper. Then use your answers to write a summary of the reading. Write your summary as a paragraph.

1. What is the title (the name) of the reading?
2. Why do people celebrate a new baby?
3. What is one American tradition?
4. What do people around the world often do to celebrate?
5. What do babies in every culture need?
6. How do babies get their names?

Sharing Opinions

Take turns answering these questions in a small group. Then share your opinions with the class.

1. Why do you think Koreans wait 100 days to celebrate a new baby?
2. Why do you think Africans plant a tree when a baby is born?
3. Is Apple a good name for a girl?
4. Is it good for a boy to have the same name as his father?

Using New Words

Work with a partner. Choose five target words or phrases from the list on page 156. On a piece of paper, use each word or phrase in a sentence.

Writing

a timeline

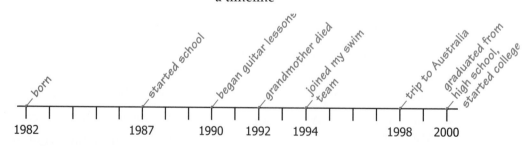

Draw a timeline of your life. Mark the important events in your life, from the day you were born to the present. Then write a paragraph about your life. You can begin with: *I was born in* _____. You can introduce sentences like this: *At age* ____, *I . . .* or *In 19*____/*200*____, *I . . .*

CHAPTER 20

Graduations

Having some fun at graduation

GETTING READY TO READ

Talk with a partner.

1. What do you see in the photo?
2. What do you think about graduation ceremonies? Circle your answer. Then give reasons for it.

   Graduation ceremonies are usually _____

   a. fun   **b.** serious   **c.** exciting   **d.** too long   **e.** _____
3. What is a good way for students to celebrate their graduation?

READING

Look at the words and pictures next to the reading. Then read.

Graduations

1   Imagine you're a senior[1] and it's your graduation day. How do you feel? Are you happy about the end of classes? Or are you sad about saying good-bye to friends? Some seniors feel ready for new experiences. Other seniors are nervous about the changes **ahead**. However, most of them agree: Graduation is a time to celebrate with friends and have fun!

2   At many U.S. high schools and colleges, seniors have a tradition of pulling pranks. Pulling pranks means causing **trouble**, but just for fun. A prank shouldn't hurt anyone. The idea is to **surprise** people and make them laugh. Seniors often pull their pranks at night, in secret. At one high school, teachers arrived on the last day of classes and found a big **sign** in front of the building. It said "FOR SALE." At another high school, some seniors **took apart** a VW,[2] carried the pieces into the school at night, and put the car back together inside the library.

3   Graduation has a serious side, too. It's a big milestone[3] in a person's life, so schools hold graduation ceremonies, or commencements. *Commence* means *begin*, and commencement marks the beginning of something new. Most graduation ceremonies in the United States follow **similar** traditions. People expect to hear the usual commencement music, and they expect speeches[4] by important guests. Some speakers **tell jokes**, but most talk seriously about the future.

4   People also expect to see the students all dressed in caps and gowns.[5] Their teachers or professors wear similar caps and gowns. The colors that professors wear tell you about their work. For example, orange **stands for** engineering, light blue is for education, and **purple** is for law.

5   The cap a student wears is called a mortarboard.[6] A tassel[7] **hangs** from the top of it. Before graduation, everyone's tassel **is supposed to** hang on the same side of the mortarboard. Then, **immediately** after a student receives his or her degree, the student moves the tassel to the **opposite** side. It's a strange tradition!

[1] a *senior* = a student in his or her last year of high school or college

[2] a *VW* = Volkswagen

[3] a *milestone* = a very important event in someone's life or the history of something

[4] a *speech* = a talk given to a group of people

[5] a student in *cap and gown*

[6] *mortarboard*   [7] *tassel*

6   After the ceremony, students often do something else with their caps. They **take** them **off** and send them flying up into the air. How did this tradition begin? Who knows!⁸ But an old joke gives one answer: Why do graduates throw their caps into the air? Because their teachers are too **heavy**.

⁸ *Who knows! = I don't think anybody knows*

Quick Comprehension Check

Read these sentences. Circle T (true) or F (false).

1. Students are always very happy at their graduation ceremony.   T   F

2. Seniors at many U.S. schools have a tradition of pulling secret pranks.   T   F

3. People often get hurt when seniors pull pranks.   T   F

4. People expect traditional music and speeches at graduation ceremonies.   T   F

5. The parents of graduating students wear caps and gowns.   T   F

6. After the ceremony, students throw their teachers into the air.   T   F

EXPLORING VOCABULARY

Thinking about the Vocabulary

Which target words and phrases are new to you? Circle them here and in the reading. Then read "Graduations" again. Look at the context of each new word and phrase. Can you guess the meaning?

Target Words and Phrases		
ahead (1)	similar (3)	is supposed to (5)
trouble (2)	tell jokes (3)	immediately (5)
surprise (2)	stands for (4)	opposite (5)
sign (2)	purple (4)	take off (6)
took apart (2)	hangs (5)	heavy (6)

Using the Vocabulary

 A These words are **about the reading**. Complete them with the words and phrases in the box.

ahead	are supposed to	purple	similar	stand for
surprise	take off	tell jokes	took apart	trouble

1. Some graduating students look forward to changes in their future. Other students are nervous about the changes _____.

2. Seniors pull pranks at night so no one can see them. They want to _____ people.

3. *Pulling pranks* means causing _____ (making problems for people), but just for fun.

4. For a prank, a group of students _____ a car. Then it was in pieces.

5. In the United States, graduation ceremonies at one school are like the ceremonies at other schools. The schools follow _____ traditions.

6. Most graduation speakers give serious talks, but some _____ to make people laugh.

7. The colors that professors wear have meanings. They _____ something.

8. The color _____ stands for law.

9. People expect students to wear caps and gowns. The students _____ wear them.

10. Immediately after their graduation, some students _____ their caps and throw them into the air.

B These sentences use the target words and phrases **in new contexts**. Complete them with the words and phrases in the box.

ahead	is supposed to	joke	purple	similar
stands for	surprise	take off	take it apart	trouble

1. Red paint and blue paint mixed together make _____ paint.

2. Everyone _____ tell the truth in court.

3. Please don't tell him we're coming. We want to _____ him.

4. He signs his name Hector E. Diaz. The *E.* _____ Eduardo.

5. Don't get into _____ with the police!

6. I'm sure the company will be a great success in the years

   _____.

7. "Did you get the _____?" means "Did you understand it? Was it funny to you?"

8. In some cultures, people _____ their shoes when they enter a house.

9. My backpack looks a lot like yours. They're very _____.

10. The bed was too big to move in one piece. We had to _____.

C **Read these sentences. Match the boldfaced target words with their definitions.**

a. Dr. Lee got a call and had to leave **immediately**. It was an emergency.

b. After you wash your clothes, do you put them in the dryer or **hang** them outside on a line?

c. Asia and North America are on **opposite** sides of the Pacific Ocean.

d. The **sign** on the door said, "DANGER—Do not enter."

e. My dictionary is a thick, **heavy** book.

Target Words   **Definitions**

1. _____ = weighing a lot (in kilograms, pounds, etc.)

2. _____ = directly across from or facing something

3. _____ = now or right away, without waiting

4. _____ = put something up so the top stays but the bottom is free to move

5. _____ = a piece of metal, wood, or paper with information in words or pictures

Building on the Vocabulary

Studying Collocations

Take off is a **phrasal verb**. Remember: Phrasal verbs have two parts: verb + particle (such as *up, out,* or *off*). A phrasal verb can have more than one meaning. *Take off* can mean *remove (something) from the body,* or it can mean *leave or go up into the air (like a plane).* The meaning depends on the context.

A Look at the phrasal verbs in these pairs of sentences. Are the meanings similar or different? Circle S (similar) or D (different).

1. a. The plane is scheduled to **take off** at 12:30.   S   D
   b. He **took off** his hat and coat.

2. a. Please **turn up** the radio. I can't hear it.   S   D
   b. I lost my keys. I hope they **turn up** soon.

3. a. We're tired, but we have **to go on** working.   S   D
   b. What's that noise outside? What's **going on** in the street?

4. a. She had a bad cold, but she **got over** it.   S   D
   b. He was sad at first. Then he **got over** it.

B Work with a partner. Discuss the meanings of all the phrasal verbs in Part A. On a piece of paper, write four sentences with the phrasal verbs.

DEVELOPING YOUR SKILLS

Reading for Details

Read these questions. Then reread "Graduations" for the answers. If the reading doesn't give the information, check (✔) *It doesn't say.*

	YES	NO	IT DOESN'T SAY.
1. Is graduation a time for celebration?			
2. Do all seniors look forward to the new experiences ahead?			
3. Do seniors pull pranks to surprise people?			
4. Did student pranks use to be more dangerous?			
5. Do all schools in the United States follow completely different traditions at their graduation ceremonies?			
6. Are students supposed to wear black shoes with their caps and gowns?			
7. Are the tassels on students' mortarboards supposed to hang on the same side?			
8. A graduation ceremony is a serious event. Do people ever make jokes about it?			

Thinking about the Main Idea

What is the main idea of the reading? Choose the best way to complete this statement.

Graduation is a time for _____.

a. pulling pranks and making jokes

b. traditional music and serious speeches

c. fun with friends and traditional ceremonies

Discussion

Work with a partner or in a small group to complete the chart.

	In the United States	In Another Culture (or Cultures)
1. How do students have fun at graduation time?		
2. What takes place at graduation ceremonies?		

Using New Words

Ask and answer these questions with a partner. Use one of the words or phrases in parentheses. Then talk about your answers with the class.

1. Do you **take off** your shoes when you enter your (room/home)?

2. What **hangs** on the walls in your (room/home)?

3. When you were a child, did you ever (get in/cause) **trouble** in school?

4. Are you (good at/bad at) telling **jokes**?

5. Think of a **sign** for the door of your (room/classroom). What should it say?

Writing

Choose an experience from your life and describe it in a paragraph. Write about one of the following:

1. Something you did to surprise someone (What did you do? Why?)

2. A graduation ceremony (Whose graduation was it? When and where did this take place?)

3. Something you celebrated with friends (What was the reason for the celebration? What did you do?)

Wrap-up

REVIEWING VOCABULARY

(A) Think about the type of words in each of these groups. Are they nouns, verbs, or adjectives? Cross out the word that doesn't belong in each group.

1. church   card   gun   ~~celebrate~~
2. hang   throw   wide   pour
3. exciting   religious   excellent   festival
4. wet   plant   heavy   thick
5. purple   news   joke   sign
6. event   let   meal   culture

(B) Complete these sentences with the words and phrases in the box. There is one extra phrase.

able to	a couple of	hand out	hang
have something in common	stand for	supposed to	take apart
take place	used to	would rather	

1. An auto mechanic can _____ a car and put it back together.
2. She _____ be heavy, but now she's thin.
3. Drivers are _____ control their cars at all times.
4. I invited him to my graduation, but he won't be _____ come.
5. She helped the teacher _____ books to all the students.
6. When will the wedding celebration _____?
7. I have several pictures. I want to _____ them on the walls of my room.
8. We _____. We both like to go fishing.
9. I don't want to go out tonight. I _____ stay home.
10. What does A.M. _____ in time expressions like 10:30 A.M.?

EXPANDING VOCABULARY

A Two words with the same meaning are called synonyms. Two words with opposite meanings are called antonyms.

What is the relationship between the following pairs of words? Check *synonyms* or *antonyms*.

	SYNONYMS	ANTONYMS
1. thick—thin		✔
2. similar—different		
3. lasted—continued		
4. narrow—wide		
5. take place—happen		
6. guest—visitor		
7. heavy—light		
8. couple—pair		
9. take off—put on		
10. wet—dry		

B A **prefix** added to the beginning of a word changes its meaning. For example, the prefix *un-* means not. So *unhappy* means *not happy*. Other prefixes can also mean *not*.

Combine the *not* prefixes and adjectives in the box. Complete the sentences with the new words.

> **un-** + common   **im-** + perfect   **ir-** + regular   **dis-** + similar   **non-** + traditional

1. *Study, live,* and *dance* are regular verbs. *Go, have,* and *make* are
   ___irregular___.

2. The farmer sells his best apples and uses the _____ ones to make apple juice.

3. They had a _____ wedding. They got married on an airplane.

4. The two brothers have _____ jobs; one is a doctor and one is a baseball player.

5. It's _____ for a husband and wife to share the same birthday.

PLAYING WITH WORDS

**Complete the sentences with words you studied in Chapters 17–20.
Write the words in the puzzle.**

Across

3. The company is throwing a party
   to m<u>ark</u>_____ his twenty-fifth
   year there.
4. He's studying the language and
   c_____ of Japan.
5. Most businesses close on
   h_____.
7. He's graduating, so let's c_____!
9. Don't tell her about the party.
   We want to s_____ her.
10. I love f_____ fruit.
11. The job will get easier in the days
    a_____.
12. I listened to the news w_____
    I ate.

Down

1. Don't swim i_____ after you eat.
2. Breakfast is my favorite m_____.
6. After we looked at the menu, our waiter
   asked, "Are you ready to o_____?"
8. When do you e_____ to graduate?
9. They s_____ the same last name.

BUILDING DICTIONARY SKILLS

A Look at this dictionary entry. Then answer the questions.

> **news**/nuz/ *n* **1** [U] information about something that has happened recently: *Have you heard (=received) any* **news about** *your job application?* | *I have some* **good/bad news** *for you.* | *an interesting* **piece of news**. **2** [U] reports of recent events in the newspapers or on radio or television . . .

- Do you see the symbol [U]? It stands for uncountable (or noncount). *News* is a noncount noun, so it has no plural form. You can say *much* or *a little news* but not *many* or *several news*.

- Does your dictionary have a symbol or an abbreviation for noncount nouns?

  ☐ Yes, it has this (symbol/abbreviation): _____   ☐ No, it doesn't have one.

B Sometimes a noun can be both a noncount and a count noun. Look at this dictionary entry.

> **ex•pe•ri•ence**[1]/ɪkˈspɪriəns/ *n* **1** [U] knowledge or skill that you gain from doing a job or activity: *Do you* **have** *any* **experience** *in the publishing business?* **2** [U] knowledge that you gain about life and the world by being in different situations and meeting different people: **In my experience,** *a credit card is always useful.* **3** something that happens to you and has an effect on how you feel or what you think: *Visiting Paris was a wonderful experience.* | *People often say they have* **had** *similar* **experiences.**

What kind of noun is *experience* in these sentences? Check (✔) *Count* or *Noncount*.

Count	Noncount	
✔	_____	1. Our visit to Québec was a wonderful experience.
_____	_____	2. Do you have any experience with computers?
_____	_____	3. Police officers have experience with guns.
_____	_____	4. Tell us about your experiences at the festival.

C Write one sentence with *experience* as a count noun and one with *experience* as a noncount noun.

1. _____

2. _____

UNIT 6

FOOD

CHAPTER 21

Comfort Food

Freedom from Want by American artist Normal Rockwell

GETTING READY TO READ

Answer these questions. Then talk about your answers with a partner or in a small group.

1. Imagine it's late at night. You're tired, but you have to study. You're hungry, too. What would you choose to eat? Name three things:

   _____, _____, _____.

2. Circle your answers.
   a. I miss food from home.   True   False
   b. People eat when they feel sad.   True   False
   c. People eat when they feel nervous.   True   False
   d. People eat when they want to celebrate.   True   False

READING

Look at the words and pictures next to the reading. Then read without stopping. Don't worry about new words. Don't stop to use a dictionary. Just keep reading!

Comfort Food

1   It's **natural** for people to eat when they're hungry. But people eat for other reasons, too. Do you ever eat because you're with friends and everyone else is eating? Do you ever eat because you feel tired, or because you are under **stress**? Many people do. People often eat to feel better. Maybe they have too much to do, or they're nervous. Maybe they're having problems in a relationship. But when people eat to feel better, they don't eat just anything. They want **specific** kinds of food. They want food that helps them **relax**. They want comfort food.

2   What is comfort food? For most people, it's food that is easy to **prepare**. It's often soft, so it's easy to eat. Eating it gives people a warm feeling. Sometimes it's a type of food that people loved as children. Maybe they used to eat it at specific times or places. Maybe it's food their mother used to make. Comfort food makes people feel, "Somebody's taking care of me."

3   Researchers at the University of Illinois did a survey[1] on comfort food in the United States. They asked over 1,000 Americans about it. They wanted to know two things: What comfort foods did people want, and when did they want them? The **results** of the survey were **rather surprising**. The researchers expected people's favorite comfort food to be warm and soft. But it wasn't. The number one food **turned out** to be potato chips.[2] Another favorite was ice cream, especially among people aged 18–34. However, not all comfort foods are snack foods.[3] **Nearly** half of the comfort foods were healthy, homemade foods, such as chicken soup and mashed potatoes.[4]

4   People of different ages want different comfort foods. There are **differences** between the **choices** of men and women, too. The survey showed that American women

[1] a *survey* = a set of questions you ask a large group of people to learn their opinions

[2] *potato chips*

[3] *snack foods* = kinds of food that people buy ready-made to eat between regular meals

[4] *mashed potatoes*

usually choose sweet comfort foods. Women in the survey mentioned ice cream most often (74% of them like it), then chocolate (69%), and cookies (66%). Even more of the men in the survey mentioned ice cream (77%). However, men choose sweet foods **less** often **than** women. American men often want hot and salty comfort foods such as soup (73%) and pizza or pasta (72%).

5   When do Americans most want comfort food? Many people think it is only for times of stress, or when someone feels **bored** or **lonely**. However, the researchers say that the opposite is true. Yes, people eat to feel better. But more often, they eat comfort foods when they already feel happy. They eat them to celebrate or reward themselves.[5]

[5] *reward themselves* = give themselves something nice because they did a good thing

Quick Comprehension Check

Read these sentences. Circle T (true) or F (false).

1.	People eat for a variety of reasons.	T	F
2.	Comfort food is food that makes you feel good.	T	F
3.	The researchers did a study of all kinds of food.	T	F
4.	Americans' favorite comfort foods are potato chips and ice cream.	T	F
5.	Men and women agree about the best comfort foods.	T	F
6.	People want comfort food most when they're sad.	T	F

EXPLORING VOCABULARY

Thinking about the Vocabulary

Which target words and phrases are new to you? Circle them here and in the reading. Then read "Comfort Food" again. Look at the context of each new word and phrase. Can you guess the meaning?

Target Words and Phrases		
natural (1)	**results** (3)	**differences** (4)
stress (1)	**rather** (3)	**choices** (4)
specific (1)	**surprising** (3)	**less . . . than** (4)
relax (1)	**turned out** (3)	**bored** (5)
prepare (2)	**nearly** (3)	**lonely** (5)

Using the Vocabulary

 These sentences are about the reading. What is the meaning of each boldfaced word or phrase? Circle a, b, or c.

1. People eat when they are hungry. That's the **natural** thing to do. Here, *natural* means:

   a. crazy, stupid   **b.** normal, usual   **c.** strange, unexpected

2. Sometimes we get hungry for a **specific kind** of food—comfort food. A specific kind is:

   a. one type and no other   **b.** any type we can get   **c.** every type there is

3. Comfort food gives a warm feeling. It helps us **relax** and feel better. *Relax* means:

   a. become calm and less worried   **b.** become big and strong   **c.** become nervous and quick

4. Comfort food doesn't usually take a lot of work. It's easy to **prepare**. *Prepare* means:

   a. hand out   **b.** take apart   **c.** make ready

5. The information from the survey was **rather** surprising. *Rather* means:

   a. more than a little   **b.** not at all   **c.** of course

6. Many of the comfort foods were snack foods, but **nearly** half of them weren't. *Nearly* means:

   a. completely   **b.** almost   **c.** ever

7. Men and women often make different **choices** in comfort food. Choices are:

   a. things they share   **b.** things they choose   **c.** things they throw

8. Men usually like salty foods. They eat **less** sweet comfort food **than** women do. *Less . . . than* means:

   a. more than   **b.** the same as   **c.** not as much as

9. Some people eat comfort food when they are **lonely**. It makes them feel less alone. *Lonely* means:

   a. tired of being with people   **b.** away from friends and feeling sad   **c.** happy and relaxed

10. Some people eat when they feel **bored**. It gives them something to do. *Bored* means:

   a. tired of having nothing fun to do   **b.** extremely busy   **c.** tired and ready to sleep

B These sentences use the target words **in new contexts**. Complete them with the words in the box.

bored	choice	less	lonely	natural
nearly	prepared	rather	relax	specific

1. They _____ a wonderful meal for their guests.

2. The wedding will take place in a couple of days. She's very nervous. She can't _____.

3. The students almost went to sleep in class. They were very _____.

4. Let's call Dave and see if he's OK. He has no family, so he gets _____ on holidays.

5. Which movie would you rather see? My first _____ would be *Dark of the Night*.

6. This is Miki's first trip away from home. It's _____ that she misses her family.

7. His new movie isn't great. It's _____ exciting than his last one.

8. I don't have any _____ plans for the weekend. I just want to relax.

9. I washed the clothes and they're hanging outside. They should be _____ dry now.

10. This box is _____ heavy. Can you help me with it?

C Read these sentences. Match the **boldfaced** target words with their definitions.

a. I expected my team to win, but it didn't **turn out** that way. It was **surprising**.

b. What's the **difference** between *lonely* and *alone*?

c. As a **result** of the dry weather, farmers had a bad year.

d. At that time of year, students are under a lot of **stress**.

Target Words   **Definitions**

1. _____ = something that makes one person or thing not the same as another

2. _____ = different from what someone expected

3. _____ = feelings of worry that go on and on and won't let a person relax

4. _____ = something that happens or follows because of something
else

5. _____ = happen or end in a specific way

Building on the Vocabulary

Studying Word Grammar

There are many pairs of adjectives that end in *–ing* and *–ed*.

- The *–ed* adjective usually describes a person. It tells how someone feels:
  I'm **surprised** to see you here!

- The *–ing* adjective describes the thing that causes the feeling:
  They told us some **surprising** news.

- The *–ing* adjective can sometimes describe a person:
  He's a **boring** speaker.

Remember: *–ed* = how someone feels;   *–ing* = the thing that's the cause

A **Complete these sentences. Use each adjective only once.**

1. **surprising/surprised:** It was a __surprising__ event. Everyone was
   __surprised__ .
   (a)
   (b)

2. **boring/bored:** What a _____ movie! I was completely
   (a)

   _____ .
   (b)

3. **interesting/interested:** He's _____ in the law. It's very
   (a)

   _____ to him.
   (b)

4. **exciting/excited:** I'm _____ about the film festival. It's going to
   (a)

   be _____ .
   (b)

5. **relaxing/relaxed:** You look very _____ and comfortable in that
   (a)

   chair. That music is nice and _____ .
   (b)

B **Write four sentences. Use -ed and -ing adjectives.**

1. _____

2. _____

3. _____

4. _____

DEVELOPING YOUR SKILLS

Scanning

Read these questions about "Comfort Food." Scan the reading and write the answers.

1. Why do people eat? Give three or more reasons.

    _____

2. What is "comfort food"? Complete this definition with quotations from the second paragraph of the reading (using the exact words):

    Comfort food is food that helps people relax. It's "easy to __*prepare*__."
    (a)

    It's also "easy _____." Eating comfort food gives people "a
    (b)

    _____ feeling," and it "makes people feel, 'Somebody's
    (c)

    _____.'"
    (d)

3. What's the number one comfort food for Americans? _____

4. Who especially likes ice cream? _____

5. What are two examples of healthy, homemade comfort foods?

    _____

6. How are men's and women's comfort food choices different?

    _____

7. When do Americans want comfort food most?

    _____

Focusing on Details

Complete the information about men in this graph. Write the kind of food in the chart. Fill in the percentage of men who mentioned it. Then, draw a similar graph for women.

Survey Results

%	Men	Women
100		
90		
80		
70		
60		
50		
40		
30		
20		
10		

ice cream 77%

Discussion

Talk about these questions in a small group. Then tell the class the results of your discussion.

1. List five comfort foods that Americans mentioned in the survey. Do people in your group like them? Complete the chart.

Common American Comfort Foods	Number of People Who Like It	Number of People Who Don't Like It	Total Number in the Group
1.			
2.			
3.			
4.			
5.			

2. Can you give the numbers as percentages? For example: *Fifty percent of the people in our group like chocolate.*

   You can also say, _____Three_____ *out of* _____six_____ *people in our group like* __chocolate__ .

3. What do you think are the favorite comfort foods in your country? Take a guess.

Using New Words

Work with a partner. Take turns asking for and giving information.

1. Name something that causes a lot of **stress**.

2. Describe your favorite way to **relax**.

3. What's the **difference** between _____ and _____?

4. Complete this sentence: It's **natural** to feel nervous when . . .

5. If you feel **lonely**, what should you do?

Writing

What happens when you are under stress? How do you feel? What do you do to feel better? Write a paragraph. You can begin with: *When I am under stress, I* . . .

CHAPTER 22

Garlic

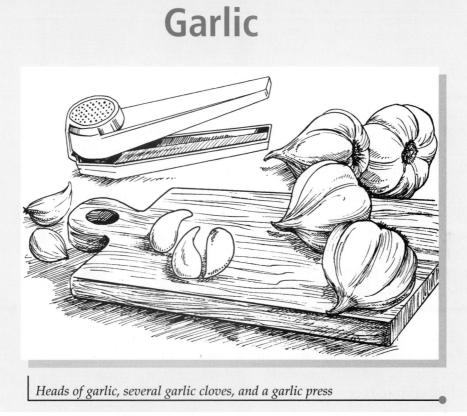

Heads of garlic, several garlic cloves, and a garlic press

GETTING READY TO READ

Answer these questions. Then talk in a small group or with the whole class.

1. How often do you eat garlic?	Often	Sometimes	Never
2. Do people in your country cook with garlic?	Often	Sometimes	Never
3. Do you think garlic is good for you?	Yes	No	I don't know

4. What kinds of food do people put garlic in? _____

_____

READING

Look at the words and pictures next to the reading. Then read.

Garlic

1   Some people can't stand garlic. "That smell! It's too strong. And it doesn't go away! There's nothing **worse than** garlic," they say. Other people say it tastes great and it's good for you, too. Chester Aaron grows eighty-seven kinds of garlic on his farm. He wrote a book called *Garlic Is Life*. It seems that people either love garlic or hate it.

2   Garlic has a long history. The first **wild** garlic **probably** grew somewhere in western Russia. People in that **area** found it and learned to use it. Later, travelers carried garlic with them to China, India, Europe, and North Africa. Farmers began planting it over 5,000 years ago. They grew garlic to eat and to use as **medicine** when they were sick. They also grew it for use in religious ceremonies.

3   People in many cultures shared similar ideas about garlic. For example, they made their slaves[1] eat it. They believed garlic made it **possible** for slaves to work harder and longer. In Greece, the athletes[2] of the first Olympic Games ate garlic. They wanted to become stronger and faster, and they believed that garlic would help. **Soldiers** in the Roman **army** ate garlic, too. They ate it to help them fight better. But garlic wasn't only for slaves, athletes, and soldiers. In some places, garlic was called "food for lovers."

4   People had even more uses for garlic. They **added** it to other foods because it tasted good. In China, people also used garlic to keep **meat** fresh. The Chinese were probably the first people to write about the uses of garlic. They wrote about garlic 4,000 years ago.

5   People in many cultures ate garlic when they got sick. It was supposed to make a cold or fever[3] go away. It was also supposed to help with different kinds of **pain**—for example, when someone's head, ear, or muscles[4] hurt.

6   Is eating garlic actually good for you, or should we just laugh at these old ideas? The truth is, doctors today are

[1] *slaves* = people who belong to someone and must work without pay

[2] *athletes* = people who do sports

[3] a *fever* = an illness that makes the body very hot

[4] strong *muscles*

telling their patients, "Eat garlic!" **Recent** research shows that garlic is good for your heart. It turns out that garlic helps people stay healthy.

7   However, we can't **accept** every idea about garlic from the past. In many cultures, people trusted garlic to protect them from all kinds of bad luck. Garlic is great, but it can't do that! Also, don't **tie** garlic around your **neck**. It won't keep vampires[5] away, as people used to think. It would probably just keep your friends away.

[5] a *vampire*

Quick Comprehension Check

Read these sentences. Circle T (true) or F (false).

1. Garlic has a long history.	T	F
2. Garlic had many different uses in the past.	T	F
3. People used to believe that garlic made them stronger.	T	F
4. People in China had no use for garlic.	T	F
5. People used to think garlic was good for them, but it wasn't.	T	F
6. Garlic brings good luck.	T	F

EXPLORING VOCABULARY

Thinking about the Vocabulary

Which target words and phrases are new to you? Circle them here and in the reading. Then read "Garlic" again. Look at the context of each new word and phrase. Can you guess the meaning?

Target Words and Phrases

worse than (1)	possible (3)	pain (5)
wild (2)	soldiers (3)	recent (6)
probably (2)	army (3)	accept (7)
area (2)	added (4)	tie (7)
medicine (2)	meat (4)	neck (7)

Using the Vocabulary

A Label these pictures. Write *meat, medicine, a neck,* and *a soldier.*

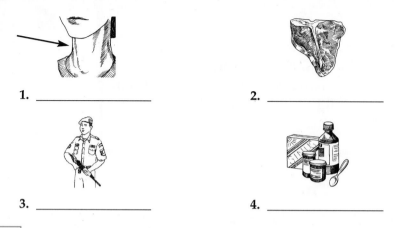

1. _____

2. _____

3. _____

4. _____

B These sentences are **about the reading**. Complete them with the words and phrases in the box.

accept	add	areas	army	pain	possible
probably	recent	tie	wild	worse than	

1. Some people say, "Nothing smells as bad as garlic. It's _____ anything else."

2. Farmers now plant garlic. But at first, garlic grew without their help. That was _____ garlic.

3. No one knows exactly where garlic first grew, but it was _____ in western Russia.

4. People from western Russia carried garlic to other _____.

5. Were slaves really able to work harder because of garlic? Did garlic make it _____?

6. An _____ is a country's group of soldiers who fight on land.

7. People sometimes want to give the taste of garlic to another food. So they _____ garlic to that food.

8. When you have a headache, your head hurts. Garlic was supposed to be good for that kind of _____.

9. We can _____ some ideas about garlic from the past, but we can't believe them all.

10. We have information from the past, and _____ research gives us new information.

11. People used to wear garlic. They would _____ it around their necks.

C These sentences use the target words and phrases in **new contexts**. Complete them with the words in the box.

accept	add	area	army	pain	possible
probably	recent	tie	wild	worse	

1. People have pets in their homes. Pets are not _____ animals.

2. Breaking a finger is bad, but breaking your arm is _____.

3. Some people _____ milk and sugar to their coffee.

4. Soldiers in the _____ are working for their countries.

5. The dentist said, "If you feel any _____, I'll stop."

6. Is it _____ to taste the differences among eighty-seven types of garlic? I'm sure I couldn't!

7. Marta and Nicolas will _____ have their wedding in a church, but they aren't sure yet.

8. The sign says this is a no-smoking _____, so people aren't supposed to smoke here.

9. We depend on TV for news about _____ world events.

10. How old were you when you learned to _____ your shoes?

11. The old woman tried to pay the boy for his help, but he wouldn't _____ any money.

Building on the Vocabulary

Studying Collocations

When a part of your body hurts, you can say:

I have a pain in my (back/neck/shoulder/leg/foot).

People don't usually say, *I have a pain in my (head/tooth/ear).* There are specific words for these kinds of pain: *I have a **headache/a toothache/an earache**.*

A Write a sentence about each picture. Tell what's wrong with the person.

1. _He has a pain in his shoulder._   2. _____

3. _____   4. _____

DEVELOPING YOUR SKILLS

Scanning

A Where is the information about these topics in "Garlic"? Scan the reading on pages 182–183. Write the paragraph number (1–7).

  _7_   **a.** advice about garlic

_____ **b.** garlic in China

_____ **c.** the early history of garlic

_____ **d.** people's feelings about garlic

_____ **e.** recent research on garlic

_____ **f.** using garlic to make people stronger

_____ **g.** garlic for sick people

B Write a sentence about each of the seven topics from paragraphs 1–7. Use information from the reading.

1. _____

2. _____

3. _____

4. _____

5. _____

6. _____

7. _____

Summarizing

A This summary of "Garlic" doesn't give enough specific information. It's too general. Each statement needs support.

People have strong feelings about garlic. It has a long history of different uses. Scientists now study garlic.

Read these sentences. Put a check (✔) next to the four sentences you want to add to the summary.

☐ People used to eat garlic to become stronger and faster.

☐ First there was wild garlic, and then farmers grew it.

☐ People also ate it for health reasons.

☐ Recent research shows that it's good for us.

☐ Some love it and some hate it.

B Where do the four sentences belong? Rewrite the summary from Part A, adding the four sentences you chose.

_____

_____

_____

_____

_____

_____

Sharing Opinions

A Read these sayings about food. Check (✔) your opinion of each one. Then share your reasons in a small group.

	It might help.	It probably doesn't help.
a. Eat garlic for thick hair.		
b. Fish is brain food.		
c. Carrots are good for your eyes.		
d. An apple a day keeps the doctor away.		

B In your country, are there any sayings like the ones in Part A about eating specific foods? Write a list with your group. Give your opinions about these beliefs.

Using New Words

Work with a partner. Choose five target words or phrases from the list on page 183. On a piece of paper, use each word or phrase in a sentence.

Writing

Choose a food topic and write a paragraph about it.

1. What is a food that is good for people's health? (What is it good for? Who says it's good? Do you eat it?)

2. What is one food that you like to make? (How do you make it? When do you eat it?)

3. Describe a food from your country. (What's it like? Do you eat it often or only at special times?)

4. Choose your own food topic.

CHAPTER 23

Wedding Cake

A three-tiered wedding cake

GETTING READY TO READ

Talk with your whole class.

1. Does the cake in the picture look good to eat?
2. When and where do people have a cake like this?
3. Do people have traditional foods at weddings in your country?

READING

Look at the words and pictures next to the reading. Then read.

Wedding Cake

1   Do you ever see American weddings in Hollywood movies? Those weddings aren't all exactly the same. They can **vary** in a hundred ways. But one thing never changes: There is always a wedding cake. You see it at the reception[1] after the wedding ceremony. In the movies, the cake is always tall, and it's always white, like the long white dress of a traditional **bride**. On top of the cake, you'll probably see a little plastic bride and **groom**.

2   At a real American wedding, things won't be just like in the movies. The bride may wear blue. But there will **definitely** be a cake.

3   When did this tradition begin? The first wedding cakes were made thousands of years ago in Greece. A wedding cake at that time was more like bread. The bride had to make it herself, and it took her two days or more. Before she baked[2] it, a child would throw a **ring** into it. Later, when people ate the bread, someone would find the ring. That person was supposed to be the next one to get married.

4   Most brides today don't bake their own cakes; they buy them. Some brides spend a lot of money on them. A wedding cake can **cost** thousands of dollars. One woman ordered her cake from a famous cake maker 2,000 miles away. Her father sent his private plane to **pick** it **up**. The bride said, "I want my cake to be special! Nobody will remember the food at my wedding, but everyone will remember the cake."

5   When it's time to cut the cake, the bride and groom do it together. The bride uses a **knife** with flowers or **pretty** ribbons[3] on it. The groom **places** his hand on hers. They cut the first piece from the **bottom** tier[4] of the cake. The bride holds the piece, and the groom takes a **bite**. Then he holds it while she takes the next bite. The bride and groom **save** the top tier of the cake and freeze[5] it. They will eat it one year later, on their first **anniversary**.

[1] a *reception* = a party for the wedding guests

[2] People *bake* bread in ovens.

[3] a cake knife with *ribbons*

[4] This cake has three *tiers*.

[5] *freeze* = make very cold so it becomes hard

6   Most guests eat their piece of the cake at the reception. But some people take it home in a box. That night, they put the box under their pillow.[6] Why? It's another tradition. When they go to sleep, they're supposed to dream of the man or woman they will **marry**.

[6] a *pillow*

Quick Comprehension Check

Read these sentences. Circle T (true) or F (false).

1. Hollywood movies sometimes show American weddings.   T   F
2. Wedding cakes in the movies are always tall and white.   T   F
3. The bride and groom stand on top of the cake.   T   F
4. Most American brides bake their wedding cakes themselves.   T   F
5. There are special traditions for how to cut a wedding cake.   T   F
6. Nobody really eats wedding cake.   T   F

EXPLORING VOCABULARY

Thinking about the Vocabulary

Which target words and phrases are new to you? Circle them here and in the reading. Then read "Wedding Cake" again. Look at the context of each new word and phrase. Can you guess the meaning?

Target Words and Phrases		
vary (1)	**cost** (4)	**bottom** (5)
bride (1)	**pick up** (4)	**bite** (5)
groom (1)	**knife** (5)	**save** (5)
definitely (2)	**pretty** (5)	**anniversary** (5)
ring (3)	**places** (5)	**marry** (6)

Using the Vocabulary

A Label these pictures. Write *a bride, a groom, a knife,* and *a ring.*

1. _____

2. _____

3. _____

4. _____

B These sentences are **about the reading.** Complete them with the words and phrases in the box.

anniversary	bite	bottom	cost	definitely	marry
pick up	places	pretty	save	vary	

1. Weddings aren't all the same. They _____ in many ways.

2. There will _____ be a cake at any wedding reception in a Hollywood movie. You can be sure of that.

3. Wedding cakes can be expensive. They can _____ a lot of money.

4. One bride's father sent his private plane to _____ his daughter's wedding cake. Someone went 2,000 miles to get the cake and bring it back!

5. When they cut the first piece of cake, the groom _____ his hand on top of the bride's hand.

6. They use a knife with flowers or ribbons on it. These make the knife look _____.

7. They cut the first piece from the _____ tier of the cake. This is the largest part.

8. The groom takes the first _____ of cake. Then the bride eats a little from the same piece.

9. They don't eat the top part of the cake. They _____ it for later.

10. One year later, the couple will celebrate their first _____.

11. Some people put wedding cake under their pillow. They hope to dream about the person that they will _____.

C These sentences use the target words and phrases **in new contexts.** Complete them with the words and phrases in the box.

anniversary	bite	bottom	cost	definitely	marry
pick up	placed	pretty	save	varies	

1. Good-looking boys or men are called *handsome*. Good-looking girls or women are called *beautiful* or _____.

2. In conversation, people use the phrase *get married* more often than the word _____. The meaning is the same.

3. They got married fifty years ago. June 10 will be their fiftieth

    _____.

4. We eat a lot of eggs because they _____ less than meat.

5. I'm sure the news will surprise him. Yes, it _____ will!

6. She tries to _____ as much money as possible in the bank.

7. I'm going to _____ Kay at the airport. Her plane is supposed to get in at 4:00 P.M.

8. A snake bit him, and the _____ nearly killed him.

9. He hung some pictures on the wall and _____ a photo of his girlfriend on his desk.

10. The days are hot and the nights are cool. The temperature _____.

11. Put heavy books on the _____ shelf and lighter ones on the top.

Building on the Vocabulary

Studying Word Grammar

The verb **marry** is often more formal than **get married**. *Marry* is less common in spoken English. *Marry* and *get married* are used in different ways:

- Use *marry* + a person: *He married his first wife in 1975.*
- Use *get married* alone, or use *get married* + *to* + a person: *They're getting married. He got married to Mary at City Hall.*

Note: You can use *marry* alone (for example, *Did they ever marry?*), but it's not common.

A Complete these sentences. Use *marry* or *get married*.

1. When did they _____?

2. He's planning to _____.

3. Will she _____ him?

4. She _____ to someone she met at work.

B Write two true sentences with *get married*.

1. _____

2. _____

DEVELOPING YOUR SKILLS

Pronoun Reference

What do the boldfaced pronouns mean in these sentences? Look back at the reading.

1. Paragraph 1: **They** can vary in a hundred ways.   _weddings in Hollywood movies_

2. Paragraph 1: You see **it** at the reception . . . _____

3. Paragraph 3: Before **she** baked it, a child would throw a ring into it. _____

4. Paragraph 4: Some brides spend a lot of money on **them**. _____

5. Paragraph 5: The groom places his hand on **hers**. _____

6. Paragraph 5: **They** cut the first piece from the bottom tier . . . _____

Summarizing

Answer these questions about the reading. Then, on a piece of paper, use your answers to write a summary paragraph. Use "Wedding Cake" as the title for your summary.

1. What is the reading about? _____

2. What does a traditional American wedding cake look like? _____

_____

3. When did the tradition of wedding cakes begin? _____

4. At a wedding reception, who cuts the cake? _____

5. What do the bride and groom save? _____

Discussion

Work in a small group. Read the statements in the chart. They are true
of many weddings in North America. Are they true of traditional
weddings in your country? Check (✔) your answers. Tell about one or
more things that are different in your country.

	Definitely	Maybe	Definitely Not
1. There is a religious ceremony.			
2. The bride and groom wear special clothes.			
3. They give each other rings to wear.			
4. There is food afterwards.			
5. There is a wedding cake.			
6. There is music and dancing.			
7. People throw rice at the bride and groom.			

Using New Words

Work with a partner. Take turns asking for and giving information. Then
tell the class something about your partner.

1. Are you **married**?
2. When (will/did) you **get married**?
3. (Do/Will) you wear a wedding **ring**?
4. How much does a traditional wedding **cost** in your country?
5. Do people celebrate their wedding **anniversaries** in your country?

Writing

Choose a topic.

1. Write a paragraph about traditional weddings in your country. Where do
   they take place? What do the bride and groom wear? Do weddings vary a
   lot? What do wedding guests do?
2. Make two lists: "Reasons to Get Married" and "Reasons Not to Get
   Married." Write complete sentences in each list.

CHAPTER 24

Slow Food

A traditional meal to enjoy

GETTING READY TO READ

Talk with your whole class.

1. What is fast food? Write a definition. Fast food is food that _____.
2. How many types of fast food can you think of? Make a list.
3. Fill in this chart.

What's good about fast food?	What's wrong with fast food?

4. What do you think the phrase *slow food* means?

READING

Look at the words and pictures next to the reading. Then read.

Slow Food

1   Italians know and love good food. It's at the heart of their culture. They don't like to **rush** through meals, either. So, many of them think that fast food is a **terrible** idea.

2   In 1986, something happened in Italy. An American fast food restaurant—a McDonald's—opened in Rome. Many Italians were surprised and angry. They thought, "This is an **attack** on Italian culture!" One man, Carlo Petrini, decided to fight back. "Fast food is the **enemy**," he said. In 1989, Petrini started a group called Slow Food. Today, about 70,000 people belong to the group. They live in forty-five countries around the world. More people **join** every day.

3   The **members** of Slow Food have many ideas in common. There are a lot of problems with food today, they say. Fast food is one of them. For one thing, it's not healthy food. Also, it's the same everywhere. "That's boring," they say. They want to keep traditional cooking with all its variety.

4   Slow Food members worry about a second problem, too. Some types of plants and animals are getting to be very rare.[1] They **include**, **for instance**, a kind of tree in Morocco, a special type of Austrian cow,[2] and wild rice in the United States. The world is in **danger** of losing them completely. Slow Food doesn't want to let them **disappear**, so they're working with farmers to keep them **alive**.

5   There's a third problem. Big companies **produce** much of our food today. They sell their products in many places, so they want products that can travel well. Big growers[3] want the kinds of fruit and vegetables that look good after a long trip. But how do their apples, lettuce,[4] and tomatoes taste? That's less important to them. So now we have more trouble finding good-tasting food.

6   Today, it's common to eat foods from far away. Food travels an average distance[5] of 1,300 miles to **reach** dinner tables in the United States. In the past, people got their food

continued

[1] *rare* = uncommon and hard to find

[2] a *cow*

[3] *big growers* = large farm companies

[4] a head of *lettuce*

[5] *average distance* = add the distances together, then divide by the number of distances

from farms and factories in their **local** area. Slow Food members say, "People should buy more local food. It's fresh, and it's part of our culture." One American, Gary Nabhan, decided to try this. For one year, all his food came from plants and animals near his home in Arizona. One local animal is the rattlesnake.[6] Nabhan ate that, too! In his book *Coming Home to Eat*, he says it tastes just like chicken.

[6] a rattlesnake

7   Fast food is reaching more and more parts of the world. But Slow Food is getting its **message** to more and more people, too.

Quick Comprehension Check

Read these sentences. Circle T (true) or F (false).

1. Good food is an important part of Italian culture.	T	F
2. The group Slow Food started after a McDonald's opened in Rome.	T	F
3. Slow Food members say fast food is boring and bad for you.	T	F
4. Slow Food members want everyone to eat Italian food.	T	F
5. Slow Food says there are too many types of food in the world.	T	F
6. Foods from big food companies usually travel long distances.	T	F

EXPLORING VOCABULARY

Thinking about the Vocabulary

Which target words and phrases are new to you? Circle them here and in the reading. Then read "Slow Food" again. Look at the context of each new word and phrase. Can you guess the meaning?

Target Words and Phrases		
rush (1)	**members** (3)	**alive** (4)
terrible (1)	**include** (4)	**produce** (5)
attack (2)	**for instance** (4)	**reach** (6)
enemy (2)	**danger** (4)	**local** (6)
join (2)	**disappear** (4)	**message** (7)

Using the Vocabulary

 A These sentences are **about the reading.** Complete them with the words and phrases in the box.

danger	disappear	include	join	local
produce	reach	rush	message	terrible

1. Italians don't want to hurry at mealtime. They don't like to
   _____ through meals.

2. Fast food doesn't seem like a good idea to many Italians. In fact, it seems
   _____.

3. Slow Food is growing. More people _____ the group every day.

4. Some types of plants and animals might all die. We are in
   _____ of losing them.

5. These endangered plants and animals _____ a kind of tree in
   Morocco and a type of Austrian cow.

6. Slow Food doesn't want these plants and animals to _____.
   The group wants them to stay.

7. People used to grow their own food. Now big companies
   _____ most of our food.

8. Food often travels far before it gets to our homes. It may travel many
   miles to _____ your dinner table.

9. Some food doesn't travel far. It comes from the _____ area.

10. Slow Food has something to say. The group wants to send a
    _____ to people.

B These sentences use the target words **in new contexts.** Complete them
with the words in the box.

danger	disappeared	including	joined	local
produces	reach	rushing	messages	terrible

1. That store is open every day of the year, _____ holidays.

2. Every morning, I listen to the news and the _____ weather
   report on the radio.

3. The plane will be taking off immediately, so we should _____ Tokyo on time.

4. Several people called, but they didn't leave any _____.

5. Don't worry, we have lots of time. You can stop _____ around and relax a little!

6. When drivers get sleepy, they're in _____ of having an accident.

7. What a _____ movie! We didn't even stay to see the end of it.

8. Tomas recently _____ an athletic club. Now he goes there to exercise.

9. We all went to the festival together, but then he _____ and we didn't see him again.

10. Argentina _____ a lot of meat, wheat, and corn.

C Read each **definition** and look at the paragraph number. Look back at the reading on pages 197–198 to find the target word or phrase for each definition. Write it in the chart.

DEFINITION	PARAGRAPH	TARGET WORD OR PHRASE
1. a use of force to try to hurt someone or something	2	_____attack_____
2. someone you are fighting in a war; the opposite of friend	2	_____
3. people who belong to a group, club, or organization	3	_____
4. for example	4	_____
5. living, continuing to be or exist	4	_____

Building on the Vocabulary

Studying Collocations

Certain **prepositions** (words like *in*, *on*, and *to*) often follow certain adjectives.

- *angry + with* or *at* (someone): *I was angry with myself. They were angry at him.*
- *angry + about* (something): *Many Italians were angry about the McDonald's.*
- *bored + with*, *excited + about*, and *interested + in*.

Write four true statements. Use adjectives + prepositions.

1. _____

2. _____

3. _____

4. _____

DEVELOPING YOUR SKILLS

Scanning

Read these questions about "Slow Food." Scan the reading and write short answers.

1. How do Italians feel about good food? _____

   _____

2. What happened in Rome in 1986? _____

3. Who is Carlo Petrini? _____

4. What do Slow Food members think about fast food? _____

   _____

5. What's in danger of disappearing? _____

6. Why don't some fruits and vegetables taste good? _____

   _____

7. How far does food travel (on average) in the United States? _____

8. What do Slow Food members think about local food? _____

   _____

9. Who is Gary Nabhan? _____

   _____

Summarizing

Complete this summary of the reading.

Slow Food is a group with members in forty-five countries. It started

because _____.

Slow Food members care about _____.

They want people to _____.

Role-playing

Form a small group. One or two of you are members of Slow Food. One or two of you are reporters for a newspaper or TV program, and you eat fast food every day. The reporter(s) ask questions. For instance, they can ask the Slow Food members about their group, their ideas about food, and what they eat. The Slow Food members answer the questions and ask the reporters their own questions.

Using New Words

Work with a partner. Choose five target words or phrases from the list on page 198. On a piece of paper, use each word or phrase in a sentence.

Writing

Choose a topic.

1. Are you a member of any group? It could be a club, a religious group, a sports team, or a group of any type. Write a paragraph. Describe the group and tell why you joined it. You can begin with: *I belong to . . .*

2. Write a conversation between a reporter and a Slow Food member or a fast-food lover. For example:

REPORTER: Excuse me. Can I ask you some questions about food?

MAN: Sure . . . .

Wrap-up

REVIEWING VOCABULARY

A Think about the meanings of the words in each group below. Cross out the one word that doesn't belong in each group.

1. soldier   army   ~~medicine~~   enemy

2. neck   groom   bride   anniversary

3. danger   attack   ring   knife

4. definitely   probably   possibly   lonely

B Complete these sentences with the words in the box. There is one extra word.

alive	bored	local	natural	pretty	recent
relaxed	specific	surprising	wild	worse	

1. I get _____ doing the same thing day after day after day.

2. *A cat* means any cat. *The cat* means one _____ cat.

3. I had some _____ news: my grandmother is getting married!

4. We both have colds, but hers is _____ than mine.

5. They traveled to East Africa to take photos of _____ animals.

6. No, he's not dead! He's _____ and well and living in London.

7. The bride and groom didn't seem nervous. They looked very

   _____.

8. It's only _____ to be afraid sometimes.

9. The bride wore a _____ white dress.

10. I'm doing better now in school. I got an *A* on the most _____

    test.

EXPANDING VOCABULARY

A Read each sentence. Decide if the boldfaced word is a noun or a verb. Write *noun* or *verb*.

1. a. They made a surprise **attack**. _____noun_____
    b. When will the enemy **attack**? _____

2. a. I took a big **bite** of my pizza. _____
    b. Don't worry, that dog doesn't **bite**. _____

3. a. Where will they **choose** to get married? _____
    b. You made a good **choice**. _____

4. a. A new car **costs** a lot. _____
    b. That city has a high **cost** of living. _____

5. a. When can I find out the **results** of my test? _____
    b. The bad weather **resulted** in several accidents. _____

6. a. I can't talk now. I'm in a **rush**! _____
    b. Don't **rush** me. I'll be ready in a minute. _____

B Remember: Collocations are words that go together. Which verb can go with all of the nouns in each group below? Use *make, prepare, reach,* and *take.*

1. _____ { a message
                   some medicine
                   a bite

2. _____ { a choice
                   a decision
                   a difference

3. _____ { the bottom
                   the moon
                   the end

4. _____ { to attack
                   to leave
                   for trouble

C Write four sentences. Use a verb + noun collocation from each group in Part B.

1. _____
2. _____
3. _____
4. _____

PLAYING WITH WORDS

There are ten target words from Unit 6 in this puzzle. The words go across → and down ↓. Find the words and circle them. Then use them to complete the sentences below.

```
N  T  U  R  N  O  U  T  M
E  W  Z  M  I  Z  V  X  E
A  R  E  A  N  P  L  B  S
R  X  K  Z  C  I  E  Q  S
L  Z  N  V  L  C  S  C  A
Y  M  X  Q  U  K  S  C  G
R  P  R  O  D  U  C  E  E
V  A  C  C  E  P  T  P  K
D  I  S  A  P  P  E  A  R
```

1. I'm sorry, but he's not here right now. Would you like to leave a
   _____*message*_____?

2. A used Toyota costs _____ than a new Mercedes.

3. The new school is almost finished. It's _____ complete.

4. We watched the plane _____ behind the clouds.

5. There are three big airports in the New York _____.

6. That factory can _____ 100 cars a day.

7. Be sure to _____ the most important information in your
   summary.

8. She won't _____ any advice from him.

9. Let's _____ a pizza on our way home.

10. I wonder how the story will end. How do you think it
    will _____?

BUILDING DICTIONARY SKILLS

A Some words have more than one meaning. Look at this dictionary entry. Then circle *save* in sentences 1–4, and find its dictionary meaning. Write the number of the meaning.

---

save[1] /seɪv/ *v*

1 ▸ **FROM HARM/DANGER** ◂ [T] to make someone or something safe from danger, harm, or destruction: *We are working to* **save** *the rain forest* **from** *destruction.* | *The new speed limit should save more lives.*

2 ▸ **MONEY** ◂ [I, T] also **save up** to keep money so that you can use it later: *I'm saving up to buy a car.* | *Brian's saved $6000 to put toward a new house.*

3 ▸ **NOT WASTE** ◂ [T] to use less time, money, energy etc. so that you do not waste any: *We'll save time if we take a cab.*

4 ▸ **TO USE LATER** ◂ [T] to keep something so that you can use it or enjoy it in the future: *Let's save the rest of the pie for later.*

5 ▸ **HELP TO AVOID** ◂ [T] to help someone by making it unnecessary for him/her to do something unpleasant or difficult: *If you could pick up the medicine, it would save me a trip to the pharmacy.*

6 ▸ **COLLECT** ◂ [T] also **save sth ↔ up** to keep all the objects of a particular kind that you can find, so that they can be used for a special purpose: *She's saving foreign coins for her son's collection.*

7 ▸ **KEEP FOR SB** ◂ [T] to stop people from using something so that it is available for someone else: *We'll save you a seat in the theater.*

8 ▸ **COMPUTER** ◂ [I, T] to make a computer keep the work that you have done on it . . .

---

1. It's hard to save. I'd rather spend! _____

2. The firefighters saved everyone in the building. _____

3. We can't wash the car. We have to save water. _____

4. Save your work before you turn off the computer. _____

B Verbs have many forms. Dictionaries almost always show the simple past tense form of irregular verbs. Look at these entries. Then write a sentence with the simple past tense of each verb.

---

bite[1] /baɪt/ *v* **bit, bitten, biting 1** [I, T] to cut or crush something with your teeth: *He bit a huge piece out of the cookie.* | *I had just bitten into the apple.* | *Be careful of the dog; he bites. . .*

---

cost[2] *v* **cost, cost, costing** [T] **1** to have a particular price: *This dress cost $75.* | *It'll cost you less to drive than to take the train.* **2** to make someone lose something: *Your mistake cost us the deal . . .*

---

1. _____

2. _____

CHAPTER 25

Teaching and Learning

Fan Hongya in class

GETTING READY TO READ

Talk with a partner or in a small group.

1. What do you see in the photo?
2. Fan Hongya goes by several names. Some people call him Hongya, and some call him Mr. Fan. Others call him Marlin. How many names do you go by? Make a list. Tell who calls you each name.
3. Think of a time of great change in your life. What happened? How did you feel at the time of this change? How do you feel about it now?

READING

Look at the words next to the reading. Then read without stopping. Don't worry about new words. Don't stop to use a dictionary. Just keep reading!

Teaching and Learning

1   Fan Hongya is standing in front of his class. His students are asking questions about China. "Mr. Fan! Mr. Fan!" they call out.[1] He smiles. "My students are full of questions," he says. "They're curious[2] about different languages and cultures. Here in America, they ask everything! My students back home don't do that—not during class. It was a big change for me."

2   Fan Hongya is from China. He teaches English in Yangzhou. For a long time, he dreamed about visiting the United States. Then his dream came true.[3] He received a wonderful **offer**. He had the chance to teach Chinese in Boston for one year. "It was a great **opportunity** for me," he says. He felt very excited.

3   He flew to Boston, and a woman from his new school came to pick him up at the airport. "Please call me Marlin," he told her. "My American teacher in China gave me this name." They left the airport and drove through Boston, and she told him many things about the city. "She was very kind to me," he remembers. "She gave me a wonderful first impression[4] of the people here."

4   A new school year **was about to** begin, so Marlin had little time to get ready. He says, "I wasn't sure what to expect in my classes. But I knew that teaching American kids[5] would be a big **challenge**." The first day of school was exciting for him, but it was also a **shock**.

5   Marlin was used to classes of fifty-five students. In his first class in Boston, there were only three students. One student already spoke Chinese well. The second knew a little Chinese. The third knew nothing. Marlin thought, "Three different **levels** in one class—how can I **deal with** this?!"

continued

[1] *call out* = say in a loud voice

[2] *curious* = interested and wanting to know

[3] *came true* = became real

[4] *first impression* = a general feeling about someone or something new

[5] *kids* = (informal word for) children or teenagers

6   His second class was big, and the students were quiet and **polite**. They seemed like Chinese students. Time passed quickly. Then **suddenly**, Marlin heard the **bell** for the end of class. He wanted to say some **final** words to his students, but they were already out the door! This would never happen in China.

7   The next few weeks were difficult for Marlin. He missed his wife and daughter, and he didn't know how to deal with his classes. He felt terrible. American students seemed completely different from Chinese students. Marlin was almost ready to **quit**. He was very **disappointed** with his "dream come true."

8   After **a while**, Marlin figured things out. He adjusted to[6] the school and his students. Now he enjoys his classes, and his students love him. He will have happy **memories** of his experience in Boston. He's looking forward to going home, but he will miss his American students—and all their questions.

[6] *adjusted to* = made small changes and got used to them

Quick Comprehension Check

Read these sentences. Circle T (true) or F (false).

1. Fan Hongya and Marlin Fan are two names for the same person.	T	F
2. Marlin teaches Chinese in China.	T	F
3. He got the chance to teach in the United States for one year.	T	F
4. His American school was exactly what he expected.	T	F
5. His wife and daughter were in Boston with him.	T	F
6. Marlin says Chinese and American students are just the same.	T	F

EXPLORING VOCABULARY

Thinking about the Vocabulary

Which target words and phrases are new to you? Circle them here and in the reading. Then read "Teaching and Learning" again. Look at the context of each new word and phrase. Can you guess the meaning?

Target Words and Phrases		
offer (2)	**levels** (5)	**final** (6)
opportunity (2)	**deal with** (5)	**quit** (7)
was about to (4)	**polite** (6)	**disappointed** (7)
challenge (4)	**suddenly** (6)	**a while** (8)
shock (4)	**bell** (6)	**memories** (8)

Using the Vocabulary

Ⓐ **These sentences are about the reading. Complete them with the target words and phrases in the box.**

a while	about to	challenge	deal with	level
memories	opportunity	quit	shock	suddenly

1. Marlin had the chance to do something special. He had the
   _____ to travel to the United States.

2. It was almost time for the new school year to begin. The school year was
   _____ start.

3. Teaching in Boston would be exciting but difficult for him. It would be a
   big _____.

4. The first day of school was extremely surprising to Marlin. It was a
   _____.

5. Marlin was in the middle of teaching. He wasn't thinking about the bell
   for the end of class. Then _____, he heard it.

6. In one class, all the students were beginners. They were all at the same
   _____.

7. Marlin didn't know what to do with his classes at first. He didn't know how to _____ them.

8. He felt terrible about his job. He was almost ready to _____.

9. After _____, Marlin figured out how to deal with his students. It took some time.

10. Marlin will remember Boston with a smile. He will have happy _____ of his experience.

B These sentences use the target words and phrases **in new contexts.** Complete them with the words and phrases in the box.

a while	about to	challenge	deal with	level
memories	opportunity	quit	shock	suddenly

1. Peter smoked for twenty years. Then last year, he _____ smoking.

2. Our dinner turned out to be much more expensive than we expected. The cost came as a _____.

3. I like to look at old photos of my friends. The pictures bring back good _____.

4. We had to rush through the station. Our train was _____ leave!

5. When you take a course, do you want it to be really easy? Or do you like a _____?

6. I can't play tennis with him. He's too good. I'm not at his _____.

7. We were in the car, driving along, and then _____, a cat ran into the street.

8. The bride and groom had trouble planning their wedding. They had to _____ many problems.

9. I waited for him at the restaurant, but he didn't come. So, after _____, I left.

10. He has a new job _____. Will he take it? He has to decide soon.

C Read these sentences. Match the **boldfaced** target words with their definitions.

a. What nice, **polite** children you have!

b. I rang the **bell**, but no one came to the door.

c. A college course usually ends with a **final** exam.

d. He was **disappointed** when nobody laughed at his joke.

e. They said, "Would you like a ride?" and I was happy to accept their **offer**.

Target Words   **Definitions**

1. _____ = last, at the end of something

2. _____ = acting or speaking in a nice way

3. _____ = a thing that makes a ringing sound (like some phones)

4. _____ = a statement from someone who wants to help

5. _____ = sad because something didn't happen (or didn't turn out well)

Building on the Vocabulary

Studying Word Grammar

Some nouns can be both **count nouns** (with singular and plural forms) and **noncount nouns** (with only one form). The meanings may be different.

A Look at the **boldfaced** nouns. Circle C (count) or N (noncount) for each one.

1. She has good **memories** from her old school.   C   N

2. He has a good **memory** for names. (He doesn't forget them.)   C   N

3. How much **memory** does your computer have?   C   N

B Complete these sentences. Use *memory* or *memories.*

1. I have a terrible _____ for numbers.

2. This computer has three gigabytes of _____.

3. She has bad _____ of learning to swim.

C On a piece of paper, write two sentences with *memory* and *memories.*

DEVELOPING YOUR SKILLS

Reading for Details

Read these questions. Then reread "Teaching and Learning" for the answers. If the reading doesn't give the information, check (✔) *It doesn't say.*

	YES	NO	IT DOESN'T SAY.
1. Did Marlin look forward to traveling to Boston?			
2. Did he have the chance to take his family with him?			
3. Did he know any Americans in China?			
4. Did he expect teaching in Boston to be easy?			
5. Are Marlin's American students interested in China?			
6. Are Chinese students usually quiet and polite?			
7. Did Marlin enjoy his first few weeks in Boston?			
8. Is Marlin teaching only two classes?			
9. Is Marlin having a successful school year?			

Summarizing

Write a summary of "Teaching and Learning." Write it as a paragraph. Include answers to these questions:

- Who is Marlin Fan (or Fan Hongya)? Where is he from? What does he do?

- What did Marlin used to dream about? What did he get the chance to do?

- What was it like at first? Why?

- How did it turn out in the end?

Role-playing

Work with a partner. Imagine that one of you is Marlin and one of you is his wife. You are talking on the phone. It is the first week of the school year in Boston. What will Marlin say about his experiences at school? What questions will he and his wife have for each other?

Using New Words

Work with a partner. Choose five of the target words or phrases from the list on page 211. On a piece of paper, use each word or phrase in a sentence.

Writing

Choose a topic. Write a paragraph.

1. What part of learning English is a challenge for you? Complete the sentence below. Then give your reasons.

   Sometimes learning English is hard. It is a challenge for me to . . .

2. Marlin will have happy memories of his trip to the United States. Do you have happy memories of a trip? Write about it. You can begin with: *I have happy memories of a trip to . . .*

CHAPTER 26

"It Was Love, So Strong and So Real"

Arunaa

GETTING READY TO READ

Talk with a partner.

1. You're going to read a love story. It's about two people from opposites sides of the world. What are some possible challenges for them?

2. How important is it for married people to have things in common? Choose a number between 1 (extremely important) and 4 (not important at all). Explain your answer.

READING

Look at the words next to the reading. Then read.

"It Was Love, So Strong and So Real"

1   Arunaa was in her last year of college near her home in Malaysia. It was the first day of a new course, and she was in class. "Suddenly," she says, "I had this **awful** feeling of being watched." She looked across the room. Someone was **staring** at her—an exchange student[1] from Europe. He went on looking at her all through the class. He did it the next day, too, and the next. **Finally**, she told herself, "Enough! I'm going to talk to him. That will stop him." So she went and sat down next to him. She **discovered** that his name was Hervé, and he was French. "As soon as we started talking, it was magic[2] and he was perfect."

2   Arunaa and Hervé **fell in love**. But after a few months, he had to return to France. Soon afterwards, Arunaa graduated and **faced** the biggest decision of her life. Hervé wanted her to join him in Paris. Should she go, or should she try to forget him?

3   Arunaa remembers, "My parents were in **total** shock. But the best thing was that they never said no. It was always my choice and my responsibility. This is what they always taught me, to make my own decisions."

4   It was hard for Arunaa to think of leaving family, friends, and home. Living in France would be a challenge, too. For one thing, she didn't speak French. "And it was difficult for me," she says, "because I wasn't really sure what to expect. When I met Hervé, he was a student, and almost like a tourist.[3] He was happy in Malaysia and he felt **comfortable** there, but that wasn't real life for him. I was about to meet another Hervé, whom I didn't know—the Hervé who was **no longer** a student, but a man with a serious job, and a Frenchman in his own country."

5   Arunaa decided to go. "I had to take the chance.[4] **Although** there were many differences between us, we were

continued

[1] *exchange student* = someone who studies for a while at a foreign university

[2] *magic* = something so special it seems impossible

[3] a *tourist* = someone who is traveling for fun

[4] *take the chance* = do something that is possibly dangerous

so much **alike**! I knew that he was the one for me." For Arunaa and Hervé, it was the right decision. Now they are happily married.

6   **Marriage** isn't easy. It's even harder when a **couple** has to deal with differences in language, religion, and culture. Arunaa says, "The cultural differences were enormous.[5] I come from an Islamic country, although my family is Christian, and many things in France shocked me." The hardest thing, she says, is to understand the way that French people think.

[5] *enormous = very, very big*

7   Smaller differences in their everyday life caused problems, too. Arunaa laughs, "We are like night and day![6] I eat rice three times a day, and I don't wear shoes in the house. Also, I want to take care of my husband, like my mother and her mother before her. But that makes Hervé uncomfortable." Even with all the **difficulties**, after two years, they **remain** very much in love.

[6] *like night and day = complete opposites*

Quick Comprehension Check

Read these sentences. Circle T (true) or F (false).

1. Arunaa is a young woman from Malaysia.   T   F

2. She met Hervé when she was a college student in France.   T   F

3. Arunaa's parents told her not to leave home.   T   F

4. Arunaa and Hervé are now married and living in France.   T   F

5. It was hard for Arunaa to get used to many things in her new life.   T   F

EXPLORING VOCABULARY

Thinking about the Vocabulary

Which target words and phrases are new to you? Circle them here and in the reading. Then read "'It Was Love, So Strong and So Real'" again. Look at the context of each new word and phrase. Can you guess the meaning?

Target Words and Phrases		
awful (1)	faced (2)	alike (5)
staring (1)	total (3)	marriage (6)
finally (1)	comfortable (4)	couple (6)
discovered (1)	no longer (4)	difficulties (7)
fell in love (2)	although (5)	remain (7)

Using the Vocabulary

(A) These sentences are **about the reading**. What is the meaning of each **boldfaced** word or phrase? Circle a, b, or c.

1. Arunaa saw someone new across the room. He was **staring** at her. *Stare* means:

   a. speak, talk　　　**b.** point a finger　　　**c.** keep looking

2. **Finally**, Arunaa said, "Enough!" She decided to speak to him. *Finally* means:

   a. immediately　　　**b.** after a long wait　　　**c.** extremely

3. She talked to him and **discovered** that he was French. *Discover* means:

   a. find out, learn　　　**b.** tell, say　　　**c.** think about

4. Arunaa had to **face** a big decision. *Face* means:

   a. take off　　　**b.** deal with　　　**c.** turn out

5. Hervé felt **comfortable** in Malaysia. It was good to be there. *Comfortable* means:

   a. stressed　　　**b.** bored　　　**c.** relaxed

6. **Although** there were differences between Arunaa and Hervé, they were similar, too. *Although* means:

   a. because　　　**b.** even if　　　**c.** as a result of

7. Arunaa says they are different in some ways but **alike** in others. *Alike* means:

   a. the same or very similar
   b. disappointed, unhappy
   c. the opposite

8. Arunaa and Hervé are married. They have a good **marriage**. *Marriage* means:

   a. a plan for the future
   b. the relationship between a husband and wife
   c. memories of the past

9. This is the story of a **couple** from two different cultures. A *couple* means:

   a. a difference in ideas and traditions
   b. two people in a relationship
   c. a problem or difficulty

10. It's not easy to be married. There are even more **difficulties** in cross-cultural marriages. *Difficulty* means something that is:

    a. fun
    b. hard
    c. new

B These sentences use the target words **in new contexts**. Complete them with the words in the box.

alike	although	comfortable	couple	difficulty
discovered	face	finally	marriage	stare

1. We looked out the window and _____ that it was snowing.

2. In my country, it's not polite to _____ at people. What about in yours?

3. _____ he's not tall, he's a good basketball player.

4. Finally, the judge said to the _____, "You are now husband and wife."

5. My parents are celebrating the twentieth anniversary of their _____.

6. You can't run away from this problem. You have to _____ it.

7. We had _____ with the math problems. It took us a long time to figure them out.

8. I was _____ in bed, and I didn't want to get up.

9. She and her sister look _____, and they wear similar clothes.

10. After six years together, Mike and Rosie _____ decided to get married.

C Read each **definition** and look at the paragraph number. Look back at the reading on pages 217–218 to find the target word or phrase for each definition. Complete the chart.

DEFINITION	PARAGRAPH	TARGET WORD OR PHRASE
1. very bad, terrible	1	_____
2. started to be in love with someone	2	_____
3. complete, including everything	3	_____
4. not now, not anymore	4	_____
5. stay, continue	7	_____

Building on the Vocabulary

Studying Collocations

- Some adjectives have a variety of uses. For instance, they can come:
  before nouns *(a big house, good luck)* OR
  after the verb *be (It was big. That's good.)*

- Some adjectives can be used in **only one way**.
  The adjective *total* always comes before a noun. For example, we say, *The news was a **total shock***. We cannot say, *That's total.*

The adjectives *following*, *main*, and *whole* can also come only before a noun. For example, we can say, *I ate the whole pizza.*

Work with a partner. Look at these adjective + noun pairs. Discuss their meanings. Then write two sentences with adjective + noun.

1. a total (surprise/failure/disappointment)

    a. _____

    b. _____

2. the main (idea/reason/difference)

    a. _____

    b. _____

3. the whole (idea/thing/world)

   a. _____

   b. _____

4. the following (message/information/day)

   a. _____

   b. _____

DEVELOPING YOUR SKILLS

Scanning

Read these questions about "'It Was Love, So Strong and So Real.'" Scan the reading. Write complete sentences to answer the questions.

1. How did Arunaa meet Hervé? _____

   _____

2. What happened after Arunaa graduated from college? _____

   _____

3. What did Arunaa's parents do? _____

   _____

4. How did Arunaa feel about going to France? _____

   _____

5. Why did she decide to go? _____

   _____

6. What difficulties did she face in France? _____

   _____

7. What kinds of differences did Arunaa and Hervé have to deal with?

   _____

Identifying Paragraph Topics

What is each paragraph in the reading about? Write the topics of the paragraphs.

1. Paragraph 1: _____ how Arunaa and Hervé met _____

2. Paragraph 2: _____

3. Paragraph 3: _____

4. Paragraph 4: _____

5. Paragraph 5: _____

6. Paragraph 6: _____

7. Paragraph 7: _____

Sharing Opinions

Talk about the following opinions in a small group. Tell why you agree or disagree.

Opinion 1: Your parents' opinion of the person you marry is extremely important.

Opinion 2: People should decide for themselves about marriage. They—and not their families—should have total responsibility for the decision.

Opinion 3: It's better to marry someone who is as much like you as possible.

Using New Words

Ask and answer these questions with a partner. Use one of the words or phrases in parentheses. Then talk about your answers with the class.

1. What is something that (tastes/smells) **awful**?

2. How do you feel when (a man/a woman) **stares** at you?

3. What is something that you **no longer** (can/want to) do? Why not?

4. What are two things that are important for a good (relationship/**marriage**)?

5. What are two of the **difficulties** of (learning a new language/meeting new people)?

Writing

Choose a topic.

1. What questions would you like to ask Arunaa or Hervé? Write a list.

2. Do you believe in love at first sight (falling in love the first time you see someone)? Write a paragraph. You can begin with: *I (believe/don't believe) in love at first sight because . . .*

3. When did you face a big decision in your life? What did you decide? How do you feel about it now? Write a paragraph.

CHAPTER 27

To Live as an Artist

Vitek Kruta talking about painting

GETTING READY TO READ

Vitek Kruta was born in communist[1] Czechoslovakia.* Work in small groups. Look at the countries in this list. Which ones have or had a communist government? Check (✔) your answers.

[1] *communist =* having total government control of all land, factories, food production, schools, etc.

		In the Past	Now	Never
a.	Russia			
b.	China			
c.	Japan			
d.	Spain			
e.	Cuba			

* In 1993, Czechoslovakia became two independent countries: the Czech Republic and Slovakia.

READING

Look at the words and pictures next to the reading. Then read.

To Live as an Artist

1   In 1981, the artist Vitek Kruta escaped[1] from his country. He left with just one little bag. "One little bag with **basic** things like a toothbrush and underwear,"[2] he remembers. He was nineteen years old at the time.

2   Vitek's home was in Prague, Czechoslovakia. He loved his country, but he couldn't stay there. The communist government wanted to put him in prison. "The government wanted total control of all **art** and music," he **explains**. "We had to have art shows in secret. My kind of painting was **against the law**. The rock music that my band played was against the law. There was no future for me there." So Vitek escaped to Germany. **The rest** of his family was **still** in Prague. After he left, the police made a lot of trouble for his father.

3   In Germany, Vitek first had to learn the language. He spoke Czech and Russian but not German. So he spent eight months at a language school. Vitek remembers that it was easy for him to understand and read German, but he couldn't speak it. Then one night, he had a dream. In his dream, he was skiing[3] in the mountains. He met another skier and started talking with him—in German! The following day, he discovered that he could speak much better.

4   Next, Vitek went on with his studies in art. He learned to restore[4] old buildings such as churches and castles.[5] Ten years later, he faced another big change in his life. He got a job offer in the United States. Vitek knew **hardly** any English, but he didn't let that stop him. He had a lot of experience learning new languages! So he and his wife, Lucie, decided to make the move.

5   Today, Vitek **leads a busy life**. He is a painter, an architect, and much more. He is a man with lots of **energy**. He works in his studio,[6] he shows his work at festivals, he teaches art classes, and he helps **manage** an art school.

continued

[1] *escape* = get away when someone is trying to catch you

[2] *underwear* = clothes you wear under your shirt, pants, etc.

[3] *skiing*

[4] *restore* = make new again

[5] a *castle*

[6] *studio* = the work place of an artist

6   Vitek also has some very big art projects. He likes to bring together people with different talents[7] and **abilities** to do these projects. Sometimes he has a group work on restoring a building. Sometimes they **cover** a room with murals (large pictures painted on the walls). Vitek likes to do these projects in **public** places—at schools, in churches, for festivals—so that anyone can see and enjoy them. Projects like these, he says, "bring art back to the people."

7   Vitek believes that art must have an important place in our lives. Art lets people be creative.[8] The world needs creative people. Vitek explains, "If we are not free to be creative—and I'm talking about scientists and mathematicians, too, not just artists—then human beings can only **copy** the past. We cannot move **forward**."

[7] *talents* = special abilities to do things well, as in music, sports, etc.

[8] *creative* = good at thinking of and making new things

Quick Comprehension Check

Read these sentences. Circle T (true) or F (false).

1. Vitek grew up in communist Czechoslovakia.   T   F

2. At age nineteen, he was in danger of going to prison.   T   F

3. Now he lives and works in the United States.   T   F

4. He likes to keep his artwork private.   T   F

5. Vitek says, "Nobody actually needs art, but it's fun."   T   F

EXPLORING VOCABULARY

Thinking about the Vocabulary

Which target words and phrases are new to you? Circle them here and in the reading. Then read "To Live as an Artist" again. Look at the context of each new word and phrase. Can you guess the meaning?

Target Words and Phrases		
basic (1)	**still** (2)	**abilities** (6)
art (2)	**hardly** (4)	**cover** (6)
explains (2)	**leads a . . . life** (5)	**public** (6)
against the law (2)	**energy** (5)	**copy** (7)
the rest (2)	**manage** (5)	**forward** (7)

Using the Vocabulary

 These sentences are about the reading. Complete them with the target words and phrases in the box.

art	basic	copying	covers	forward
hardly	manage	public	the rest	still

1. Vitek left Czechoslovakia with only a few _____ things. These were simple but necessary things, such as a toothbrush.

2. The government of Czechoslovakia wanted to control all forms of _____. They wanted artists to paint only specific kinds of pictures.

3. Vitek was the only one of his family to escape. _____ of his family remained behind.

4. When Vitek left, his family was _____ in Prague. They continued to live there.

5. Vitek knew _____ any English before moving to the United States. He knew almost none.

6. Today Vitek helps _____ an art school. He is one of the decision-makers for the school.

7. Vitek sometimes paints murals. A mural is a large painting that _____ a whole wall. It is painted directly on the wall.

8. Vitek likes to do art projects in _____ places (places that anyone can enter).

9. Vitek says people have to be free to be creative. Being creative means thinking of new things, not just _____ things from the past.

10. He believes human beings shouldn't stay as we are now. We should move _____ with new ideas.

B These sentences use the target words and phrases **in new contexts.** Complete them with the words in the box.

art	basic	copy	covered	forward
hardly	manages	public	the rest	still

1. She owns and _____ the company. Ten people work for her.

2. A VCR has buttons for *play, stop, rewind,* and *fast* _____.

3. Snow fell during the night. It completely _____ the ground.

4. There is no smoking in any _____ school building in the state.

5. I saw the first part of the movie. Then I fell asleep and missed _____ of it.

6. The university has a great collection of Japanese _____.

7. The message was very short. It _____ said anything.

8. All human beings share certain _____ needs, such as air, water, and food.

9. When you _____ someone's exact words, put quotation marks ("/") around them.

10. He has been a member of the club for twenty years. He joined the club twenty years ago, and he is _____ a member.

C Read these sentences. Match the **boldfaced** target words with their definitions.

a. His parents discovered his musical **ability** when he was very young.

b. The children were full of **energy**, and they played for hours in the park.

c. I don't understand the homework. I'll ask the teacher to **explain** it.

d. Children can't drive. It's **against the law**.

e. They now **lead a** happy married **life** together.

Target Words   **Definitions**

1. _____ = live a (specific kind of) life

2. _____ = something that a person can do

3. _____ = the power of body and mind that lets you be active and do things

4. _____ = talk about something so it's clear and easy to understand

5. _____ = in disagreement with or opposed to government rules

Building on the Vocabulary

Studying Word Grammar

Hardly and *hard* are very different.

> *He works **hard**.* = He's a hard worker; he puts a lot of energy into his work.
> *He **hardly ever** works.* = He works very little. He almost never works.

Hardly usually comes before the main verb. It has a negative meaning *(almost not)*. Do not use it with another negative word. *(I hardly never see her.)*

 A **Rewrite these sentences using *hardly*.**

1. We almost couldn't see the plane. ___We could hardly see the plane.___

2. I almost can't hear you. _____

3. He almost never cries. _____

4. They almost never speak in class. _____

B **Write two sentences with *hard* and *hardly*.**

1. _____

2. _____

Scanning

Read these questions about "To Live as an Artist." Scan the reading and write answers in complete sentences.

1. Who is Vitek Kruta? _____

2. Why did he leave Czechoslovakia? _____

   _____

3. When did he escape? _____

4. Where did he go first? _____

5. Where does he live now? _____

6. What languages does he know now? _____

   _____

7. What are three examples of the type of work Vitek does? _____

   _____

8. Why should art have an important place in people's lives? _____

   _____

   _____

DEVELOPING YOUR SKILLS

Thinking about the Main Idea

What is "To Live as an Artist" about? Write one or two sentences that give the main idea of the reading.

_____

_____

Discussion

Talk about these questions in a small group.

1. Some people leave their countries because they don't have any other choice. Do you know anyone who had to leave his or her country? Tell what happened.
2. Think about going to live in another country without knowing the language. What is the hardest part of a move like that?
3. Does art have a place in your life? Explain.

Using New Words

Work with a partner. Take turns completing these statements. Then share information about your partner with the class.

1. Superman has the **ability** to fly. I wish I had the **ability** to . . .
2. For **the rest** of my life, I want to . . .
3. I can't **explain** . . .
4. I think . . . should be **against the law**.
5. People shouldn't . . . in **public** places.

Writing

Do you know someone who had to leave his or her country, someone who has a special ability, or someone who leads an interesting life? Write a paragraph about this person. You can begin with: _I want to tell you about . . ._

CHAPTER 28

An Amazing Woman

President Ruth Simmons

GETTING READY TO READ

Talk in a small group or with your whole class.

1. What kind of life do you imagine the woman in the photo has?

2. You will read about big changes in Ruth Simmons's life. You will also read about changes in the United States during the last fifty years. Think about your country fifty years ago. What is one thing that is now very different? Complete this sentence:

Fifty years ago in my country, _____,

but now _____.

READING

Look at the words and pictures next to the reading. Then read.

An Amazing Woman

1   Ruth Simmons was born in a very poor family. Today, she's the president of a famous American university. How did she do it? It's an **amazing** story.

2   The story begins on a farm in Grapeland, Texas, in 1945. Ruth was born that year. Her parents were farmworkers, and she was the youngest of their twelve children. They weren't able to give the children many things, and Ruth never had any **toys**. For Christmas, she didn't receive any **presents** at all **except** a shoebox with an apple, an orange, and some nuts.[1] However, in Grapeland, Ruth wasn't really **aware of** being poor. Then the family moved into the city, to Houston. In the city, being poor was much harder.

3   Ruth's mother kept the family together. She had no education, "but she was very **wise**," Ruth remembers. "She taught us about the real **value** of being a human being, what mattered and what didn't matter." Ruth's mother didn't have big dreams. She just wanted to see her children grow up. This was not a simple wish. At that time, there was segregation[2] in the United States. Life was dangerous for African Americans, especially in the South.[3] Ruth remembers living in **fear**. "If you looked at someone the wrong way, you could be killed."

4   At age five, Ruth fell in love with school. She was a **bright** child, and she was lucky to have some excellent teachers. No one in Ruth's family had much education, but her teachers **encouraged** her to go to college, and Ruth was **brave** enough to try. They also gave her money and even a coat to wear.

5   At first, Ruth studied theater.[4] But what kind of career could she have? She says, "Remember I grew up in the South; I couldn't even go to theaters."[5] So she studied languages instead. Later, she married, had two children, and began a career as a college teacher and administrator.[6] Soon people began to **notice** her and respect her abilities.

[1] *nuts*

[2] *segregation* = laws that kept black people from using the same schools, hotels, restaurants, etc. as white people

[3] *the South* = the southern states where whites had black slaves from the 1600s until 1863

[4, 5] *theater* = 1) reading, writing, and acting in plays; 2) a place where you see a movie or a play

[6] an *administrator* = a manager in the government, a school, a business, etc.

6   In 1995, Ruth became president of Smith College, a famous American college for women. Ruth was the first African American to **lead** a college like this one. Suddenly, her story was on TV and in newspapers all over the country. Six years later, she accepted another challenge. She became the president of Brown University.

7   Ruth believes in the **power** of education. "Learning can be the same for a poor farm kid like me as it is for the richest child in the country. It's all about cultivating one's mind,[7] and anybody can do that. So it doesn't matter what color your **skin** is, it doesn't matter how much money your father has, it doesn't matter what kind of house you live in. Every learner can experience the same thing." As President Simmons will tell you, education can change your life.

[7] *cultivating one's mind* = helping your mind to grow

(President Simmons' words come from "Poised for the Presidency" by Judith Gingerich and Sarah Curran Barrett, Smith Alumnae Quarterly, *Winter 1995/96. The final quotation has been simplified.)*

Quick Comprehension Check

Read these sentences. Circle T (true) or F (false).

1. Ruth Simmons is the president of a famous American University.   T   F

2. She grew up in a very poor family.   T   F

3. While she was growing up, she always planned to go to college.   T   F

4. She grew up during a dangerous time for black Americans.   T   F

5. She always wanted a career as a college president.   T   F

6. Ruth's message is, "Education can change any person's life."   T   F

EXPLORING VOCABULARY

Thinking about the Vocabulary

Which target words and phrases are new to you? Circle them here and in the reading. Then read "An Amazing Woman" again. Look at the context of each new word and phrase. Can you guess the meaning?

Target Words and Phrases		
amazing (1)	wise (3)	brave (4)
toys (2)	value (3)	notice (5)
presents (2)	fear (3)	lead (6)
except (2)	bright (4)	power (7)
aware of (2)	encouraged (4)	skin (7)

Using the Vocabulary

A These sentences are about the reading. What is the meaning of each **boldfaced** word or phrase? Circle a, b, or c.

1. Ruth Simmons has led a very unusual life. Her life story is **amazing**. *Amazing* means:

   a. common and expected
   b. surprising and wonderful
   c. ordinary and boring

2. Ruth's family was poor, and she never got any **presents** as a child. A present is:

   a. something one person gives to another
   b. an idea for something fun to do
   c. something to eat or drink

3. At first, being poor didn't matter. Ruth wasn't **aware of** being poor. *Aware of* means:

   a. happy about and proud of
   b. excited about and interested in
   c. knowing and understanding about

4. Although she had no education, Ruth's mother was very **wise**. *Wise* means:

   a. able to make good decisions
   b. afraid of many things
   c. polite to other people

5. She taught her children the true **value** of things in life. The value of a thing is:

   a. where it comes from
   b. its history
   c. how much it's worth

6. Ruth and many other African Americans lived in **fear** of being killed. Fear is:

   a. the feeling of being afraid
   b. a memory of something
   c. a place or an area

7. Ruth was a **bright** child, so she did well in school. *Bright* means:

   a. hungry   **b.** intelligent   **c.** angry

8. She was nervous about college. She had to be **brave** to try it. *Brave* means:

   a. ready to face danger   **b.** too afraid to do   **c.** crazy, like a fool
                           something

9. People **noticed** Ruth's abilities and respected her work. *Notice* means:

   a. produce or make it   **b.** become aware of   **c.** joke about

10. Ruth now **leads** a famous American university. She is the president. *Lead* means:

    a. study or learn   **b.** discover or find out   **c.** show others what to do

B These sentences use the target words and phrases **in new contexts.**
Complete them with the words and phrases in the box.

amazing	aware of	brave	bright	fear
lead	noticed	presents	value	wise

1. Many Americans bring a tree into their house at Christmas. They put
   _____ under the tree for family members.

2. He's a fast learner. He's very _____.

3. People expect soldiers to be _____.

4. I wasn't _____ the problem. Please explain it to me.

5. The boys _____ the pretty girl and kept staring at her.

6. We all understand the _____ of a good education.

7. People often go to him for advice. He's a very _____ man.

8. You can speak six languages? That's _____!

9. You know the way, so you _____ and we'll follow.

10. Many people are afraid to fly. Many others have a _____ of
    public speaking.

C Read these sentences. Match the **boldfaced** target words with their definitions.

a. I **encourage** her to call us if she has any problem.

b. The president has the **power** and the responsibility to lead the country.

c. She has light **skin**. It burns easily in the sun.

d. The little boy received some **toys** and games as birthday presents.

e. Everyone is here today **except** Jamal. He's sick.

Target Words   **Definitions**

1. _____ = things for children to play with

2. _____ = not including, besides

3. _____ = the ability to control or affect people and events

4. _____ = the natural covering of a person's (or an animal's) body

5. _____ = say or do things to help a person feel confident enough to do something

Building on the Vocabulary

Studying Word Grammar

Some adjectives, such as *aware, alike, afraid,* and *alive,* cannot come before a noun. Use these adjectives after *be.* For example:

He **was aware** of the difficulty. The two cars **were** exactly **alike.**
They**'re afraid** of dogs. Her grandmother **is** still **alive.**

We cannot say, *The afraid dog ran under the table.*

Rewrite these sentences with *be* + *aware, alike, afraid,* and *alive.*

1. The manager knows about it. _____ *The manager is aware of it.* _____

2. She has a fear of flying. _____

3. Everyone lived after the accident. _____

4. I didn't know about the problem. _____

5. Our backpacks are the same. _____

DEVELOPING YOUR SKILLS

Reading for Details

Read these questions. Then reread "An Amazing Woman" for the answers. If the reading doesn't give the information, check (✔) It doesn't say.

	YES	NO	IT DOESN'T SAY.
1. Was Ruth Simmons born in the United States?			
2. Did she have younger brothers and sisters?			
3. As a child, was she aware of dangers for black Americans?			
4. Did she enjoy and succeed in school?			
5. Did Ruth's parents encourage her to go to college?			
6. Did her teachers help her go to college?			
7. Was planning a career in theater a wise idea for her?			
8. Did she study at Harvard University?			
9. Was she the first woman to lead a famous college in the United States?			
10. Was her story on TV?			

Summarizing

Write a summary of "An Amazing Woman." Write it as a paragraph. Include the answers to these questions:

- Who is Ruth Simmons?
- Where did she grow up?
- What is unusual about her life story?
- What does she believe in?

Discussion

Talk about these questions in a small group.

1. Ruth's teachers encouraged her to go to college. Who encourages you? What do they encourage you to do? Why?

2. Ruth has strong ideas about what's right and what's wrong, and what matters and what doesn't matter. She learned these values from her mother. Where did you learn your values? How did you learn them?

Using New Words

Work with a partner. Choose five of the target words in the list on page 234. On a piece of paper, use each target word in a sentence.

Writing

Choose Discussion question 1 or 2 from above. Write a paragraph. You can begin with:

1. _____ *encourage(s) me to* _____. *(He/She/They) always tell(s) me* . . .

2. *I learned my values from* _____. *(He/She/They) taught me to* . . .

Wrap-up

REVIEWING VOCABULARY

(A) Match the words in the box with their definitions. There is one extra word.

ability	difficulty	fear	memory
offer	opportunity	power	present

1. _____ = something that causes problems
2. _____ = the feeling of being afraid
3. _____ = ability to control, lead, or change people or things
4. _____ = something you remember from the past
5. _____ = a chance or the time that it's possible to do something
6. _____ = a skill, power, or talent that not everyone has
7. _____ = a statement that someone is ready to help

(B) Complete the sentences below. There are two extra words or phrases.

about to	aware of	basic	challenge	deal with	forward
level	no longer	notice	remain	the rest	

1. They _____ live here. They moved to another apartment.
2. I know you're under a lot of stress. How do you _____ it?
3. The class is _____ end. We have just two more minutes.
4. The first part of the book was very good, so I read _____ of it.
5. Her parents aren't _____ the relationship. It's a secret.
6. Please _____ in your seats until the pilot turns off the "Fasten seat belt" sign.
7. She got her hair cut, but her husband didn't _____.
8. Everyone needs _____ skills in reading, writing, and math.
9. They are both beginners. They are at the same _____.

EXPANDING VOCABULARY

A A **suffix** is an ending for a word. Adding a suffix to a word can change it from one part of speech to another. The suffix *–ment* is added to some verbs to form nouns:

> Lawyers **argue** in court. (verb)
> He had an **argument** with his wife. (noun)

Add the suffix *–ment* to each of the verbs in the box. Complete the sentences with the nouns.

agree	amaze	disappoint	encourage	excite	manage

1. I watched in ___amazement___ as the man climbed up the side of the tall building.
2. The movie was a _____. We expected it to be better.
3. The two sides finally reached an _____.
4. We're looking forward to all the _____ of the holidays.
5. The other members of the team gave me _____ before my race.
6. His sons take care of the day-to-day _____ of the company.

B **Complete the chart with the boldfaced members of each word family.**

1. a. These are **comfortable** shoes.
   b. The mother **comforted** the child.
   c. The hotel tries to offer all the **comforts** of home.

2. a. Please **lead** the way.
   b. She's an experienced **leader**.
   c. What's the **leading** cause of car accidents?

3. a. What a **shocking** story!
   b. The news came as a **shock**.
   c. She **shocked** her parents with her green hair.

4. a. He lost a **valuable** ring.
   b. I **value** your opinion very much.
   c. His research is of great **value** to heart patients everywhere.

NOUNS	VERBS	ADJECTIVES
		comfortable

PLAYING WITH WORDS

**Complete the sentences with words you studied in Chapters 25–28.
Write the words in the puzzle.**

Across

4. They're brothers, but they don't look alike_____.

6. The scientist d_____ a new star.

8. She hates her job. She wants to q_____.

9. Soccer players need a lot of e_____.

10. A city park is a p_____ place.

11. I can h_____ hear you.

12. They invited everyone e_____ me!

Down

1. A_____ he was tired, he went on studying.

2. A baby has very soft s_____.

3. Don't look! Close your eyes and c_____ them.

5. Firefighters are b_____.

7. She was born in Seoul, and she s_____ lives there.

10. Parents teach their children to be p_____.

BUILDING DICTIONARY SKILLS

A Many words have more than one meaning. Which meaning does *bright* have in each sentence? Write the number of the meaning.

1. The sky was a **bright** blue. _____

2. He's a **bright** boy. _____

3. The sun is very **bright** today. _____

> **bright** /braɪt/ *adj* **1** shining strongly or with plenty of light: *a bright sunny day* | *bright lights* **2** intelligent: *Vicky is a very bright child.* | *a bright idea* **3** bright colors are strong and easy to see: *Her pants were bright red.* **4** cheerful: *a bright smile* **5** likely to be successful: *You have a bright future ahead of you!* **6 bright and early** SPOKEN very early in the morning . . .

B Which meaning does the **boldfaced** word have in the sentence? Write the number of the meaning.

1. She **manages** a clothing store. _____

2. How did you **manage** to fix the TV? _____

> **man•age** /ˈmænɪdʒ/ *v* [I, T] **1** to succeed in doing something difficult, such as dealing with a problem, living in a difficult situation: *It was heavy, but I **managed to** get it up the stairs.* | *I don't know how we'll manage* (=how we'll buy the things we need) *now that Keith's lost his job.* **2** to direct or control a business and the people who work in it: *Managing a hotel . . .*

3. Brazil played in the **final**. _____

4. History is my **final** class for the day. _____

5. Are you ready to take your **finals**? _____

6. That's my **final** offer. Take it or leave it. _____

> **fi•nal**[1] /ˈfaɪnl/ *adj* **1** last in a series of actions, events, or parts of something: *the final chapter of the book* **2** unable to be changed or doubted: *Is that your final decision?* | *No more cookies, **and that's final**!*
>
> **fi•nal**[2] *n* **1** the last and most important game, race, or set of games etc. in a competition: *She skated very well in the final.* | *the NBA finals* **2** an important test that students take at the end of each class in HIGH SCHOOL or college: *How did your finals go?*

Vocabulary Self-Test 2

Circle the letter of the word or phrase that best completes each sentence.

1. We _____ rain, but the weather was fine.
   - **a.** expected
   - **b.** copied
   - **c.** marked
   - **d.** placed

2. My visit to your country was a wonderful _____.
   - **a.** army
   - **b.** bite
   - **c.** enemy
   - **d.** experience

3. I'm not sure who did it, but it was _____ Dan.
   - **a.** immediately
   - **b.** nearly
   - **c.** probably
   - **d.** terribly

4. The girls _____ a pizza and two drinks from the waiter.
   - **a.** joined
   - **b.** ordered
   - **c.** tied
   - **d.** varied

5. I don't want to go out. I _____ stay home.
   - **a.** deal with
   - **b.** take off
   - **c.** turn out
   - **d.** would rather

6. The president has a difficult job. He's under a lot of _____.
   - **a.** ability
   - **b.** area
   - **c.** stress
   - **d.** toys

7. The players got _____ in the rain.
   - **a.** alive
   - **b.** heavy
   - **c.** thick
   - **d.** wet

8. Let's not walk. Let's take a taxi instead. It will _____ time.
   - **a.** lead
   - **b.** save
   - **c.** notice
   - **d.** throw

9. Would you please _____ some water for me?
   - **a.** cost
   - **b.** hang
   - **c.** pour
   - **d.** marry

10. Don't _____ the cat go outside.
   a. accept
   b. explain
   c. cover
   d. let

11. There are too many things in the bag. It's _____ break.
   a. about to
   b. similar to
   c. supposed to
   d. used to

12. How long did the movie _____?
   a. last
   b. add
   c. rush
   d. share

13. The patient told the doctor, "I have a _____ in my back."
   a. guest
   b. pain
   c. ring
   d. sign

14. After the game, we were hungry, so we went out for a _____.
   a. church
   b. joke
   c. meal
   d. shock

15. I have happy _____ of our trip to the beach last summer.
   a. challenges
   b. differences
   c. medicines
   d. memories

16. He just started to study Spanish, so he's at the beginning _____.
   a. choice
   b. level
   c. member
   d. result

17. Yesterday wasn't a _____ school day. The students got out early.
   a. lonely
   b. narrow
   c. pretty
   d. regular

18. There was snow all over the mountain, from the top to the _____.
   a. bottom
   b. holiday
   c. present
   d. soldier

19. A wedding is an important _____.
   a. attack
   b. danger
   c. event
   d. message

20. It's _____ to feel sad when your friends go away.
   a. local
   b. natural
   c. perfect
   d. recent

21. The government has a lot of _____ over people's lives.
    a. bride
    b. moon
    c. power
    d. skin

22. The teacher _____ the students to tell their stories.
    a. disappeared
    b. encouraged
    c. handed out
    d. took place

23. He's a good swimmer. He has no _____ of the water.
    a. fear
    b. knife
    c. meat
    d. value

24. I wasn't _____ of the change in the schedule.
    a. aware
    b. basic
    c. public
    d. wild

25. France _____ hundreds of kinds of cheese.
    a. reaches
    b. surprises
    c. relaxes
    d. produces

See the Answer Key on page 246.

VOCABULARY SELF-TESTS ANSWER KEY

Below are the answers to the vocabulary self-tests. Check your answers, and then review any words you didn't remember. You can look up the word in the index on the next two pages. Then go back to the reading and exercises to find the word. Use your dictionary as needed.

Vocabulary Self-Test 1 (Units 1–4; pages 135–138)

1. c	7. c	13. a	19. b	25. c	31. c
2. b	8. b	14. b	20. d	26. d	32. d
3. a	9. a	15. a	21. b	27. c	
4. c	10. d	16. d	22. a	28. a	
5. d	11. a	17. b	23. d	29. a	
6. d	12. c	18. c	24. b	30. b	

Vocabulary Self-Test 2 (Units 5–7; pages 243–245)

1. a	6. c	11. a	16. b	21. c
2. d	7. d	12. a	17. d	22. b
3. c	8. b	13. b	18. a	23. a
4. b	9. c	14. c	19. c	24. a
5. d	10. d	15. d	20. b	25. d